The Ties That Bind

A Wiccan View of Religious Pluralism

Philip B Terry-Smith, Ph.D., Th.D.

The Ties That Bind
A Wiccan View of Religious Pluralism

Copyright © 2012 by Philip B Terry-Smith
All Rights Reserved. Printed in the United States of America. No part of this book may be used, printed or reproduced in any form or by any electronic, mechanical, or other means, now known or hereafter invented, including photocopying, recording and information storage and retrieval, without the written permission of the author and publisher except in the case of brief quotations embedded in critical articles and reviews or academic discourse.

Photo Credit: Royalty Free Stock Photos, Microsoft clip art or Original Photography .
All original photography © 2012 PB Terry-Smith

    ISBN-13   978-0-9885429-2-1 (paper back)
    ISBN-13   978-0-9885429-3-8 (ebook)

Distributed by Lulu

For bulk distribution:
info@marceycreekpublishing.net

http://www.marceycreekpublishing.net

The Ties That Bind

A Wiccan View of Religious Pluralism

Philip B Terry-Smith, Ph.D., Th.D.

Marcey Creek Publishing™

Dedication and Acknowledgements

I am first thankful and grateful to the Divine Creator, the God and Goddess manifest that has and always brings blessings to my life. This study has been a long time coming. I can trace its roots back to my childhood, back to the days of singing in the choir and belonging to the youth ministry team at Morning Star Baptist. In those days, I felt Spirit and knew there was something much deeper than what was on the surface. I made the decision very early on to quest and find that deeper meaning and, unbeknownst to many, my dear late great grandmother whet my taste for deeper meaning by her subtle introduction to her native ways, that followed by the introduction (albeit at a very elementary stage) to native spirituality and questing through an ordeal in my youth (those that know-know!) my path was clear. A deeper understanding of spirituality and a life time of study to explore humanity and our social interactions, the world in which we live, and the universe in which we dwell would be a significant part of my personal journey. To that extent, I must give honor to my first spiritual mentor, the Rev. Dr. Samuel Ray and my great grandmother Bertha Howell for setting me on such a diverse and wonderful quest.

I dedicate this to the women that have shaped my understanding of the Goddess manifest; my mother Tamara Byrd and grandmother Helen Chase; academic mentors Dr. Rosemary Madl-Young, Jernice Lea, Mapula Ramashala, and the late Dr. Violet Plants; Spiritual advisors

Arianna Lightening Storm, Dolores Ashcroft- Nowiki, Deidre Corban Arthen, Sue Arthen, Selena Fox, Margot Adler and the late Ladys Circe, Alexandria, and Sintana. I dedicate this to the men who epitomize the God-force, my father Dr. Raymond Terry Sr., my late uncle Troy Jerome Lewis; spiritual advisors and first co-walker on this path, Orion Foxwood, R.J. Stewart, Andras Corben Arthen, James Welch and Ivo Dominguez, Jr., Jeremiah; academic mentors Dr. Robert Loring, Rev. Dr. Tom Snowden, Dr. Lilburn Hoehn, the late Dr. Robert DeHaan. I dedicate this to the memory of so many who have gone before but remain dear in my heart. Finally, I dedicate this to the individuals who have been a pillar and spiritual rock in my life as I have moved through some of the darkest moments, H. Alexander Satorie-Robinson, Gregory Satorie-Robinson, and most of all, my husband and present co-walker Justin B. Terry-Smith who knows me more than any other! And to our son, an old soul with a spirit of wonder

~*May the Divine shine blessing to each who have been guiding lights on my journey.*

About the writer

Philip B. Terry-Smith is a licensed professional counselor, ordained Interfaith Chaplain and Wiccan Elder/Priest with over 28 years of experience in helping people and organizations realize their full potential and achieve life goals. He has studied with and trained under the auspices many of the most renowned spiritual teachers of indigenous and nature based religions. He has had the honor of learning many spiritual traditions.

He has practiced in the field of human services since 1985. His specialties have included human development, organizational systems, community organizations and humanitarian care.

His work helps move individuals to healthier, more fulfilling relationships with self and others. Through his Path Awareness(tm) philosophy, he offers a unique approach to providing coaching and mentoring for personal, professional and spiritual growth and achievement, as well as counseling and guidance to foster a healing spirit and *at-one-ment*. Regardless of faith or belief, his working can assist you in establishing or building a strong connection with spirit and a path to the life you wish to live.

He holds a Doctorate of Philosophy in social systems (social/psychology) and a Doctor of Sacred Theology degree. He is advancing his studies in law toward a Doctor of Laws in International Humanitarian and International Public Law. He is a commissioned officer in the 10th Medical Regiment of the Maryland Defense force and was a volunteer responder to the Sept 11th 2001, terrorist incidents at both the Pentagon and New York where he served as a Red Cross Mental Health Officer. He holds the honor of Eagle Scout and was recognized as one of the "Outstanding Young Men of America."

He serves as adjunct faculty for the graduate programs at Lincoln University of Pennsylvania and the School for Public Service Leadership, Graduate Studies at Capella University as well as for the Sociology Department of Anne Arundel Community College in Maryland and has been a featured lecturer at virtually every major university in the Baltimore/Washington Area.

When he's not working, teaching or volunteering, he can be found in studio creating or producing music with other artists, facilitating productions as the Director or technical consultant, or creating via photography. His love for music and technical gadgetry presents an avocation for which he is quite fond. He created and produced the Pagan Music Festival for many years and was the Technical Director and productions coordinator for previous music focused Heartland Pagan Gatherings amongst others. He currently resides with his spouse Justin and their son in Laurel, Maryland.

Table of Contents

Dedication and Acknowledgements ii

About the writer iv

List of Figures and Tables xi

Forward by Orion Foxwood xii

Introduction 1

Historical context of the major religions of the world 4

East Asian Origins 5

    Chinese Traditions 5

    Confucianism 7

    Japanese Traditions 7

Near East/ Indian Origins 9

    Buddhism 9

    Hinduism 10

    Jainism 11

    Zoroastrianism 12

Sikhism	13
Near East/Indian	14
Tantra	14
Abrahamic Origins also known as the "blood religions"	16
Geographic Origins of the Abrahamic Faiths	16
Judaism	17
Christianity	19
Islam	20
Indigenous Religions	22
Australia	23
Pacific and Oceania	24
Korea	24
Africa	25
Afro-Brazilian	27
Afro-Caribbean	27
North America	29

South America 30

　　　European Religions 32

　　　The Ancient Celts 33

　　　Germanic Indigenous 33

New Religions 35

　　　Baha'i 36

　　　Christian Science 36

　　　ISKCON (Hare Krishna) 37

　　　Jehovah's Witnesses 37

　　　Scientology 38

　　　Unitarian-Universalism 39

　　　New Age 40

　　　Paganism (Neo-paganism) 41

　　　Wicca 43

Faith, Society and the Individual 48

　　　Religion the Social Institution 48

> Religion: the Pillar 61
>
> Gender, Race and Age Differences 67
>
> Religious trends and a mixture of faiths 71

Understanding Belief and Religious Faith Convergences 81

> The Convergence 81
>
> The Shared 85
>
> The Experience 92

The Path from Diversity to a Pluralistic Society 98

> The Ethical Richness 108

Moving forward 111

List of Figures and Tables

Figure 1 Historical Time Line of Religious Evolution...................47

Figure 2 The Open Systems Model..51

Figure 3 The Interdependence of Components..........................59

Figure 4 Man and Religion...60

Figure 5 Relative Comparison of Adherents................................63

Figure 6 Distribution of U.S. Religious Adherents.......................65

Figure 7 Comparison of Religiously Unaffiliated by Generation...70

Figure 8 The Spiral..96

Table 1 Number of US Adherants...64

Table 2 The Rules of 10..110

Foreword

It is at once a joy and a pleasure to write this forward for Dr. Philip Terry-Smith's *The Ties that Bind: A Wiccan View for Religious Pluralism*. I have known Dr. Terry-Smith for nearly 30 years and have watched him consistently seek the ways and means to be an active agent of positive changes in multiple sectors of our world ranging from public health, social education, clinical practice and eco-spiritual development. His tireless quest to affect the human spirit's capacity to be a healing, helping and innovative presence within the planetary ecology inclusive, but not limited to, the human quest, is a gift to us all. In this book, he brings together all of the elements of his professional, clinical, academic and spiritual development into what can best be termed as a literary platform for social and spiritual change.

Terry-Smith leads the reader on a journey through the treasures of the time honored "roots" of major world religions and innovative and need-responsive "wings" of the new ones. He walks us through a brief, concise and useful introduction to these religions, their basic philosophies and areas of both agreement and conflict. This type of journey was very insightful for me as both a Seer and a Witch because it invites us not to just see the world from where we stand but to look through the eyes of the human global culture as a "truth-journeyer". He makes it clear that our need for the re-linking and contextual offerings of religion is likely a permanent fixture in human cultural and personal development. He also helps us see that the fresh and time-responsive qualities of emerging religious movements that give contemporary insight merged with support to older practices keeping humanity current with the growth of its own spirit.

There are many unique treasures offered by Terry-Smith in this document such as: an algorithm and time-line of religious spiritual discovery and revelation up to the current time; the application of the systems approach to the emerging and changing need of the spiritual domain of human experience; the pattern of religion as a time-specific response to a human need for context and integration; information on the changing "religious landscape" that illustrate a personal and direct relationship with the forces of wholeness that we call Creator (God, Goddess, Great Spirit etc.); and his "rules of ten", which is a presentation of the cross-religions directives and philosophical foundations. This list only names of few of the treasures herein.

As the neo-pagan, earth-religions and Wiccan movement continues to grow and evolve, so does our challenge to concurrently understand our offerings to the philosophical world while embracing the worth of core teachings in other faiths. As he eloquently points out, the neo-pagan community is already rising up to this challenge. I invite and implore the reader of this book to take seriously Terry-Smith's invitation for pluralism and a movement from the battlefield of dogma onto the dancing floor of pluralistic spiritual paradigm. This dancing-floor is a place where we can share commonality, mutuality and a potential camaraderie in our quest for spiritual context and wholeness that is integrative, restorative and healing of inner, outer and societal conflict. It is a place where tolerating our differences is not enough to heal us. They must be explored and celebrated. We must consider moving from the homogeneity of the great melting pot to the delicious integration of the great soup pot where each flavor balances and augments the other. The pluralism illustrated in *The ties that Bind* is an invitation to unity, peace and healing.

Orion Foxwood

Orion Foxwood is a conjurer in the American southern folk tradition, a traditional witch, and a Faery Seer. He is the founder of Foxwood Temple of the Old Religion in Maryland and the House of Brigh Faery Seership Institute, and a co-founder of Conjure Crossroads and the annual Folk Magic Festival held in New Orleans. For over 25 years he has lectured extensively and been a media and public presence on southern conjure, witchcraft, folk magic, Faery practices, and other magical and spiritual subjects. He is the author of two books, The Faery Teachings and The Tree of Enchantment; and the DVD's Introduction to Faery Seership, Introduction to Southern Conjure, and Orion: On the Goddess; and a collaborative CD project with RJ Stewart, Faery Seership. He was born and raised in the Shenandoah Valley in Virginia. Visit him online at: www.orionfoxwood.com

"I do not want my house to be walled in on all sides and my windows to be stifled. I want all the cultures of all lands to be blown about my house as freely as possible. But I refuse to be blown off my feet by any." **~Mohandas K. Gandhi**

Introduction

Throughout the millennia, man has struggled with the appreciation of diversity of thought and action. It goes without saying then that our struggles have been fraught with wars, battles, persecutions and discriminations. Indeed we have used our faith differences, religions and paths as a means of establishing dominance, superiority and other means of creating stratification in an already overly stratified world. As DiZerega (2001) offers, "there has been no lack of animosity and mistrust between those of the Christian faith –one of the world's largest religions—and those of the Pagan Way –one of the world's oldest spiritual paths" (p. iii) There have historically been epic battles between the adherents of the Abrahamic faiths. Any travel to the Middle East, Jerusalem in particular, merely demonstrates this truth.

Dirks (2004), posits that it is not uncommon for there to be a strong opinion and manner of faith towards our own beliefs and an equally strong disdain to the beliefs of others. Further, Dirks (2004) offers, "any other belief would be a mockery of our own" (p. 249). While this discord is reality, the truth is that there are more similarities in belief then are often revealed and certainly manners of faith and ethics often demonstrate significant universal principles.

Ralph Emerson Waldo offers the following;

"In the matter of religion, people eagerly fasten their eyes on the difference between their own creed and yours; whilst the charm of the study is in finding the agreements and identities in all the religions of humanity." **~Ralph Waldo Emerson, unk.**

Perhaps, our world would best be served by these guiding words from Gandhi;

"It is the duty of every cultured man or woman to read sympathetically the scriptures of the world. If we are to respect others' religions as we would have them respect our own, a friendly study of the world's religions is a sacred duty." **~Mohandas K. Gandhi, unk.**

This writing intends to manifest the words of Gandhi through the "friendly study of the world's religions". In it the following questions shall be explored:

1) What is the brief historical context of the major religions of the world including: East Asian Origins, Indian Origins, Abrahamic, Western and indigenous, New Religions?
2) How does faith impact society and the individual?
3) Where do our beliefs and faiths converge?

4) How can those convergences be incorporated into a broader understanding for adherents of Wicca and Pagan theologies?

It would be pretentious to assume that these questions would be answered in full. As a reader, you can expect that these questions will only form new questions for you; indeed the intent is to provoke thought and dialogue, an exchange of ideas and ultimately, a step closer to a true pluralistic, respectful and embracing society. Read these words in that spirit; embrace these words in that context. Honor the truth that lies within and honor the truth that shall be revealed in you.

Historical context of the major religions of the world

There are tomes of research and data on the ancient beliefs structures of Egyptians, Romans and Greeks and, in fact, many polytheistic and pantheistic reconstructionist beliefs today draw from these rich traditions. Bowker (2006) asserts that there are no civilizations past or present without some form of religion as religion seems to be an integral part of all human existence. We also know that there has been a wealth of archeological discoveries that lead us to believe that there were organized forms of worship and certainly reverence and ritual that predates recorded history. Conversely, Pye (n.d.) shares,

> "The fascinating religions of ancient cultures have often died away with those cultures themselves. Examples here are the religions of ancient Egypt, of ancient Greece and the Roman Empire, and of the sophisticated cultures of South and Central America such as the Incas, the Aztecs and the Maya. In some cases we have been bequeathed a rich mythological literature or astonishing monuments such as the pyramids of Egypt or Central America. Religions which have disappeared still exercise strong fascination on our imagination, stimulating us to think about the

nature of the universe and the passage and destiny of human life within it". (Retrieved from: http://www.philtar.ac.uk/encyclopedia/introd.html

For the purpose of this study, we shall not venture back that far, but instead pay homage here to those profound beliefs and thus concentrate our efforts on those that have proceeded from approximately the 1st millennia Before Common Era (B.C.E.). Significantly, there are a number of indigenous cultural religions, beliefs and traditions that evolved over time and predate many of the religions offered herein but were transmitted only as oral traditions and through custom but never recorded. Unfortunately, many have died, but save a few customs or beliefs that have assimilated into other traditions. This analysis will present some of what is known of those valued traditions as well as explore those indigenous paths that continue to exist.

East Asian Origins

Chinese Traditions

Religions of East Asian origins are some of the oldest organized religions known to man. The only recorded belief systems to proceed East Asian traditions are those of the ancient cultures alluded to in the preceding section. Perhaps the oldest of these storied East

Asian traditions are those that evolved from Chinese culture and teachings.

The beginnings of the Chinese traditions are traced to the early 1st and 2nd millennia B.C.E. The founders were known to be cultural heroes credited with the invention of the essential human functions: writing, fire, and agriculture. Its structure mirrored the divine hierarchies of clan ancestors. These ancestors were believed to be able to predict and even control events on earth. Chinese beliefs are animistic in that natural forces such as the sun, moon, earth, rivers, and mountains were also worshipped. It is widely believed that the Chinese religion both begun and evolved within the country. The only noted outside influence on the belief structure was Buddhism which came from India in the first millennium Common Era (C.E.). There are three traditions or religions of sorts that emerged from the influence of early Buddhism: Daoism, Confucianism, and Buddhism as currently practiced. The traditions and folk customs co-existed, grew and evolved often providing the impetus to shape or influence the each other.

As the first millennium B.C.E. drew to a close, Chinese religion grew more independent of the ruling class clan. Throughout this period the dominance of the three traditions shifted based on ruling dynasty and region. There were periods where Buddhism and/or Daoism were closely allied with the government. As nationalism and later communism governments replaced the dynastic rulers, religious organizations were often persecuted and many religious works of art and temples were destroyed.

Oracle bones were the earliest noted forms of sacred text. Others included narrative histories, poetry, and records of ritual and significant events. (Retrieved from http://www.patheos.com {n.d.})

Confucianism

Circa 500 B.C.E., Confucianism emerged in China. There are some that hold that this is not a religion as there are no deities or lessons on the after-life. This faith however, according to Bowker (2006), is the dominant ethical influence on the social and religious traditions in both China and Japan. The name of the founder/philosopher, 'Confucius', is a Latinization of Kung Futzu, Master Kung. This title was attributed to Jesuit missionaries in China (Richey, J. retrieved from www.patheos.com {n.d}). For many centuries, state rituals in China were influenced by Confucianism. And perhaps most importantly, Confucianism was very instrumental in shaping Chinese social relationships and moral thought. Hence, it is offered as and considered a religion even without deities and a vision of salvation; Confucianism, as a tradition serves the same roles as comparable religions in other cultures.

Japanese Traditions

Much like China, religions in Japan emerged from long histories in which beliefs and practices surfaced from both imported and indigenous sources. The oldest indigenous beliefs formed Shinto. (Pye, n.d., Retrieved from http://www.philtar.ac.uk) This earliest form was based on feelings of awe toward the sacred powers (kami) that brought life to the earth and human community. Kami or deities are thought to inhabit sacred places in Japan.

During the 6th century CE, Buddhism was introduced into Japan; it both influenced Shinto beliefs and practices and also incorporated Shinto elements. Taoism and Confucianism both migrated to Japan, thus impacting culture, philosophy, politics and religion. Some of the influence included the adaptation of Buddhist rituals (Chinese in particular). The Taoist practices of story-telling and divination, as well as concepts of piety and ancestor veneration from Confucianism. From this, some offer that the "divine descent" of the ruling imperial clan, and thus the Emperor's power and authority, were confirmed and ordained. While there is strength in many of the traditions, there are fears that much of the religious and spiritual heritage unique to Japan is being swallowed by modern secular life.

Near East/ Indian Origins

Buddhism

Hardy (n.d.) asserts that as viewed through the eyes of historians, Buddhism emerged in northern India in the 5th century B.C.E. Its traditions trace back to Siddhartha Gotama (sometimes spelled Gautama), typically referred to as The Buddha; Buddha means literally the Enlightened (Awakened) One. Siddhartha Gotama was a wealthy prince born in India in the 6th or 5th century B.C.E. He was said to have renounced his wealth and power to quest for and find enlightenment.

Buddhist beliefs have touched virtually every quarter of the earth. Its teachings and practices have been incorporated into any number of religions particularly in the traditions of both China and Japan. In each place Buddhism has spread, it has assimilated local practices and beliefs. The Buddha's core teachings are often offered as the Four Noble Truths, which are said to come from the first sermon Siddhartha Gotama delivered after attaining enlightenment. Further teachings come from the Eightfold Path, which provides a basic guide for how one should live life. Preserved originally as a oral tradition, Buddhist doctrine contain a record of the Buddha's teachings as well as structures for social organization. As stated by Hardy (n.d.), as Buddhism evolved through the centuries, many more systematic philosophies and stories of devotion were added.

Hinduism

Sanatana Dharma, "The Eternal Teaching", are the collection of sacred texts that serve as the foundations of Hinduism. Kinnard (n.d.), suggests that Hinduism has neither a "specific marker of origin nor a specific founder", but being thought to have always existed -- as the tradition understands itself to be timeless. Thus Hinduism is a collective term applied to the many philosophies and traditions native to India. Kinnard (n.d.), further asserts that Hinduism is a complex tradition that encompasses a number of interrelated practices and doctrines that share common characteristics but are absent a single unified system of beliefs.

There are major sects as well as countless sub sects in this belief structure. As such, one could view these as distinct religious traditions, often with very specific theologies and ritual traditions. However, these sects are often understood to be different means to reach a common end. The worldview of this tradition is essentially grounded in the doctrines of the cycle of rebirth (samsara) and the universal law of cause and effect (karma). In this belief it is fundamentally held that one's thoughts and actions have a direct influence on both one's current life and future lives.

Jainism

The Indian religion Jainism dates to the 6th century B.C.E. and derives its name from the jinas ("conquerors"). Gunn (n.d.) offers that the title "jinas" was given to twenty-four tirthankaras (great teachers) through which the faith was revealed. Accordingly, Mahavira, the last of the tirthankaras, is considered the founder of Jainism. Jainism belief espouses a multi-layered universe containing both heavens and hells. Ones progression through these levels of the universe requires adherence to doctrines that emphasize a life of discipline and peacefulness.

As a belief system, the ultimate goal of Jainism is the liberation of the jiva (the self) from rebirth. Such liberation is achieved by cleansing and removing the accumulated karma which results from previous actions. {note the similarity to Hinduism articulated above}. The purging or removal of karma manifests through the concurrent control of bodily passions and a disciplined cultivation of knowledge. Once the passions have been conquered and karma removed, you become a Jina ("conqueror"). As Jina, you are no longer reborn (reincarnated). Some of the core principles of this religion are: non-violence in all parts of life (verbal, physical, and mental), detachment from material things, sexual monogamy, and speaking truth. Jains, as suggests Gunn (n.d.), are typically strict vegetarians and most often adhere to an arduous practice of non-violence. This practice of non-violence extends to the types of occupations one may follow, e.g. no farming as insects can be inadvertently harmed in the process.

Zoroastrianism

The followers of the Persian prophet Zoroaster created the ancient Iranian, pre-Islamic religion now referred to as Zoroastrianism. It was called for a time in the 19th century "Mazdaism". This religion emerged in the 6th century B.C.E. Zoroaster, also known as Zarathustra, (c.) was said to have had visions of a creator God, Ahura Mazda. This God was considered wholly good, who is opposed by the evil being Angra Mainyu. The dualism of good versus evil (which is played out in the struggle and battle between Ahura Mazda and Angra Mainyu) is the basis for Zoroastrian belief.

Similar to other paths, there is little or no distinction between the physical and the spiritual realms. As a result, Zoroastrians have a strong ethical tradition as the personal struggle of good and evil in humans is thought to have significant cosmic ramifications. Core to the belief is that each individual has the responsibility to fight against evil. The primary sacred text of Zoroastrianism is the *Avesta* ("Book of Law"), which includes hymns, festivals, guidance, rituals, and ways to cast out demons. It was for a time the official religion of three successive empires in Iran from 550 B.C.E. to 642 C.E. The religions nearly disappeared after the emergence of Islam but there remain some small communities scattered throughout the Middle East. (Retrieved from http://www.patheos.com/Library/Zoroastrianism.html {n.d.})

Sikhism

Gill, Mann, Mulhern, and Kinnard (n.d.), contends that the Sikh tradition was founded by Guru Nanak near the late 15th century C.E. in the Punjab region of what are today India and Pakistan. Guru Nanak spread a new message about the divine, which developed into the Sikh religion. Further, according to Sikh beliefs, the same spirit inhabited not only Guru Nanak but his nine successors as well. This spirit is believed to be found in the teachings of the Guru Granth Sahib, the foundational scriptures of the tradition. Some of the earliest Sikh traditions challenged the more rigid forms Hinduism, as well as the self-denying ideologies of other religious groups. Its founders desired to create lasting institutions around worship that could be shared by all people.

Sikhs, according to Gill et. al. (n.d.), reject the idea of divine incarnations and as such hold that the liberation of the soul results from being absorbed into divinity. Also rejected is the typical social doctrine of the caste system in India. Sikhs adhere to practices of equality in worship and life.

Near East/Indian

Tantra

The term Tantra encompasses a number of rituals and philosophies that emerged in India in the 7th century C.E. amongst followers of Hinduism and Buddhism. It is a vast system of practices of the esoteric nature that is helpful in achieving spiritual fulfillment.

Buddhist Tantric traditions are often referred to as "Tibetan Buddhism", while Hindu Tantric traditions emphasize the goddess power (the Shakti). The practices incorporate both the sacred texts of Hinduism and Buddhism. These texts are called "The Tantras". Patheos.com suggests that Tantra is understood as a quick path to overcoming both the attachments and desires that keep one stuck in the cycle of rebirth or *samsara*. Tantra does so by conquering the things that cause attachment and not avoiding them. For this reason according to Patheos.com (n.d.), "it is also a potentially dangerous path which, if not practiced under the guidance of a tantric expert, can lead to being consumed by one's desires". (Retrieved from http://www.patheos.com/Library/Tantra.html)

In modern times the Tantric practices have become popular in the West. Unfortunately many western versions of the tradition are seen by tantric adepts as incorrect and distorted. Ultimately these practices are seen as perversions of the philosophical and ritual principles of the tradition and thus dangerous.

Abrahamic Origins also known as the "blood religions"

The Abrahamic religions, recognized collectively as the largest among the major world religions are very closely related in their origins. They are also closely related in beliefs, sacred texts and scriptures, and institutions of leadership. (Douglas, n.d.) Similarly, there are correlations in the perspective and view of the individual and social life and in beliefs about morality. While there are a number of similar beliefs, there are also equally disparate aspects of their belief structures. Douglas (n.d.) posits that the history of relations between these faiths has been one of cooperation as well as significant conflict. Further, Douglas (n.d.) suggests that in modern times the followers of these paths seem more alien and pure enemies, while at other times they more closely resemble the squabbling children of a single parent with a greater capacity to reach understandings and live together in peace rather than battle. This proclivity to see others as alien (ethnocentricity) or enemies has been a primary source of wars and persecutions. Vaughns (n.d.), for this reason, refers to the Abrahamic traditions as "the blood religions".

Geographic Origins of the Abrahamic Faiths

Abraham lived during the Iron Age, around 2000 B.C.E., in Mesopotamia. While accounts of his life vary greatly, Douglas (n.d.) asserts two common threads: Abraham (or

Abram) was called by God to go with his family to another place and that Abraham was the ancestor and patriarch of most of the prominently the Semitic tribes that included the Hebrews, Ethiopians, and Arabs. His descendants included the major prophets of the monotheistic tradition. Abraham and his descendants settled what is referred to as the Holy Land, the region on the eastern Mediterranean coast between Mesopotamia and Egypt. In modern days, that area includes all or part of several countries, including: Palestine, Jordan, Saudi Arabia, Yemen, and parts of Egypt, Iraq, Syria, and Israel. Ironically, this is also the region of the world were significant conflict has and continues to exist. It is the land described in the scriptures of the Qur'an and Bible. The monotheistic tradition Abraham practiced evolved into the religions of Judaism, Christianity and Islam. The prophets mentioned in the Torah, the Bible, and the Qur'an were born and lived in this region. One of the core common beliefs of these traditions was that God made a covenant or agreement with Abraham to keep the faith in One God and teach the practice of worship to his children down the generations; In return, God would preserve, protect and multiply his children. What follows will be a description of each of the Abrahamic traditions.

Judaism

Krell and Nadler (n.d) suggest that the traditions of Judaism date back nearly four thousand years and are rooted in the ancient near eastern region of Canaan. This region is now known as Israel. Further, Krell and Nadler (n.d.) offer that Judaism was originally the beliefs and practices of the people known as "Israel". As such rabbinic Judaism (classic) was not prevalent until the 1st century C.E.

The patriarchs Abraham, Isaac, Jacob, and the prophet Moses are noted figures in this tradition. Moses, as history reflects, received God's law, the *Ten Commandments* known to both Judaism and Christianity at Mt. Sinai. The traditions, as articulated in the Torah, the sacred text, are grounded in the religious, ethical, and social laws. Judaism tends to emphasize practice of tradition and spirituality over belief. One of the driving premises is that God would make direct descendants of Abraham and thus those of Judaism a sacred people and give them a holy land. Those of Jewish tradition refer to the first five books of the Hebrew Bible as the Tanakh, an acronym for the texts of the Torah, Prophets, and Writings. Other sacred texts include the Talmud and Midrash, the rabbinic, legal, and narrative interpretations of the Torah.

According to Krell and Nadler (n.d.), there are four primary sects within the tradition: Orthodox, Conservative, Reform, and Reconstructionist, who respectively range from stark traditionalism to liberal to progressive (religiously) in the interpretation and application of the Torah. While there is diversity of view there is unity on the basis of their common connection to sacred text that defines their relationship with God as the *holy people*.

Christianity

It was through the influences of the Greeks and Romans in the 1st century C.E. that gave rise to the tradition called Christianity. Davies-Stofka (n.d.), proffers that Christianity was founded in the teachings of Jesus, and while propagated throughout the Roman Empire in the later 1st Century C.E. by enthusiastic evangelists, the faith was principally established in the land of Jerusalem. It is based on the life, teachings, death, and resurrection of Jesus Christ; the adherents are called "Christians."

Traditions of this faith hold the belief in the one and only "true God", that one being exists as Father, Son, and Holy Spirit. Further the belief holds that God sent his one and only Son, Jesus, as the divine (and human) Messiah to save the world. The Holy Bible is the sacred text and consists of the Hebrew Scriptures (the Old Testament) and the New Testament, which represents the recordings and teachings of the disciples (first followers) of Christ.

The three major branches of Christianity are Roman Catholic, Eastern Orthodox, and Protestantism; there are numerous subcategories within each of these branches. Each branch of this faith path offers variety in beliefs and practices. Most adherents of Christianity through the latter part of the 20th century were primarily in the West. It has spread to every continent and is now the largest religion in the world. There is much contention about the spread of Christianity and actions associated with the spread including the often violent institutionalization of faith and the annihilation of indigenous traditions and people in the name of salvation. Evangelism is the source of much of this proselytizing practice. Finally, Davies-Stofka (n.d.) shares that central to Christian practice "is the gathering at churches for worship, fellowship, and study, and engagement with the world through evangelism and social action".

Islam

The newest of the Abrahamic religions is Islam. Developed in the Middle East in the 7th century C.E Islam is also a monotheistic religion. According to Davies-Stofka and Fadel (n.d.), Islam translates literally to "surrender" or "submission". The tradition was founded on the teachings of the Prophet Muhammad which espoused surrender to the will of the creator and sustainer of the world, Allah. Davies-Stofka and Fadel (n.d.) further assert that central to the teachings of Islam, Allah is the one and true God with no partner or equal. The sacred text for this tradition is the Qur'an.

Islam has three divisions, known respectively as the Sufi, Sunni, and Shi'a; each of these subsets has differing means to maintain religious authority. Khalek, Mulhern and Kinnard (n.d.) shares that Sufism for instance has "become the general term for the mystical or esoteric expression of Islam". It is not really clear but it is believed that Sufism emerged as early as the 1st or early 2nd century after the existence of Islam—that would be the late 7th or 8th centuries C.E. It is suggested that Sufism has its beginning in the life and times of Muhammad but was heavily influenced by ascetic practices attributed to Byzantium and the Near East.

There is one major unifying characteristic of Islam-- the Five Pillars. These five practices include a ritual profession of faith, ritual prayer, the zakat (charity), fasting, and a pilgrimage to Mecca (the hajj). Davies-Stofka and Fadel (n.d.) contend that the "Five Pillars" are the fundamental practices of Islam. Accordingly, one characteristic of many Muslims is their commitment to praying to Allah five times a day.

Finally in Islam, all aspects of a life are to be oriented to serving Allah and there is no stark distinction drawn between the religious and secular aspects. From the birthplace in the Arabian Peninsula, Islam expanded immediately, with significant influence in Asia, Europe and North America.

Indigenous Religions

Grim (n.d.) alludes to the qualifying considerations that one must make in any discussion of indigenous religions. "The term "indigenous" is a generalized reference to the thousands of small scale societies who have distinct languages, kinship systems, mythologies, ancestral memories, and homelands". There are some 200 million people throughout the world that make up these small scale societies. Accordingly, these societies are extremely diverse and do not constitute what Grim (n.d.) refers to as "world religions" as one would view Christianity or Buddhism.

Of the many core beliefs inherent in indigenous paths, the one stands out most is the almost universal awareness of the integral relationship of symbolic and material life. Ritual practices and the ideals which provide structure and order to society cannot be separated out from the daily living practices as with institutionalized religions. Thus Grim (n.d.) contends "the term, 'lifeway', emphasizes this holistic context that grounds the traditional environmental knowledge evident in the cosmologies of indigenous peoples... in this sense, to analyze religion as a separate system of beliefs and ritual practices apart from subsistence, kinship, language, governance, and landscape is to misunderstand indigenous religion".

Australia

The Aboriginal practices of native Australia, espouse a worldview articulated as *Dreaming,* or *The Dreamtime*. This practice is a complex set of ideas that incorporate most aspects of life including ones past, present, and future. Conversely, Patheos.com (n.d.) offers "*Dreaming* helps orient oneself with nature, the community, and the spirits through the engagement of the spiritual realm using altered states of consciousness. All aspects of life (birth, puberty, death, etc.) have specific rituals that orient oneself to *Dreaming*."

These aspects of life are celebrated with rituals that include puberty rites, circumcision, body-piercing, scarring, and various fire rituals. Sacred art, often in the form of painting and wood carving, is another important aspect of many indigenous Australian religions. The form and style of the art depends on the cultural region. There are many forms to the beliefs and practices of the Aboriginals. These vary greatly based on region.

One very common thread however is the veneration and worship of ancestors. These regional indigenous traditions all hold that the ancestors become supernatural beings who continue to interact with the living. Additionally, related to the veneration of ancestors, most of the groups also believe that ancestors can be reincarnated as newborns within the family. Another common thread to the Aboriginal practices is that of song, dance, and mythology which enables adherents to access to the spiritual world and help unify the cosmic order.

Pacific and Oceania

Oceania Religions include the plethora of beliefs and practices of those who inhabited the Pacific Islands, specifically the South Pacific. These Oceanic traditions are generally polytheistic, with a worldview that embraces both the spiritual and natural worlds. Typically there is little or no distinction between that of the supernatural and the natural. They are animistic as well; many believe that spirits inhabit objects such as rocks, sticks, tools, and buildings. Rituals and ceremonies are not just for religion, but also have specific consequences in and for the natural and supernatural worlds.

There is significant deviation in these traditions as the language and culture from one place to the other are very diverse. Despite such diversity, there are a number of commonalities that a shared. Patheos.com (n.d.) shares, for example, that pregnancy, war, agriculture and wealth are all believed to be influenced by spiritual beings. Conversely, it is also believed that an individual has supernatural power that can be added to or taken away.

Korea

Historically, both culture and religion in Korea has been influenced by several other traditions ranging from

Islam to Christianity, Buddhism, Confucianism as well as Taoism. Those influences however do not negate that there are also unique religious beliefs and practices in Korea that are rooted in indigenous practices and ancient Siberian and central Asian shamanistic traditions. As such the indigenous Korean Religion speaks to the ancient native agricultural and shamanistic traditions unique to that land. These traditions include animal and sun symbolic and a number of mythologies that describe the formation of the Korean land and people. Of these traditions one of the most well-known myths is that of the semi-divine man/animal, Tan' gun, who became the god of the Korean state. (Retrieved from www.patheos.com/Library/Korea.html {n.d.})

These traditions also have strong components based on the cycles and harvest rituals that are also equated to agricultural and human fertility. These rituals include magic, healings, and exorcisms, and were traditionally conducted by shamans and kings. Native Korean beliefs also adopted many Confucian principles of ethics and manner of living.

Africa

African Indigenous refers to the large and diverse number of religions native to the continent of Africa. Further for this discourse, the term African Indigenous Religion will refer specifically to the religions indigenous to those areas within Sub-Saharan Africa that have less influence by interactions with Asia and Europe. For simplicity, this discussion will also include an examination of the indigenous traditions of the Caribbean and Brazil. While the regions of the Caribbean and Brazil likely had customs and traditions of their own respectively, the evolutions of those traditions were heavily influenced by the introduction of African beliefs that imported with the Trade Wind slave industry.

There is a wide variety of religions and beliefs on the continent of Africa, those beliefs are as diverse and disparate as the political and social environments in which they developed. Like so many indigenous religions, the traditions, teachings, mythology and legends are passed on by oral exchange and few were recorded in the means of a sacred text. Patheos.com (n.d.) suggests that most African religions have creation mythology and a host of wisdom proverbs that are the basis of political and societal order.

African traditions have a variety of deities in addition to the Supreme God; typically, these deities are animistic and reflect different aspects of nature such as rain, the sun, agriculture, and animals as well as the cosmos. The veneration of the ancestors is also usually a significant aspect of African traditions. In addition, some of the Sub-Saharan customs employ magick, divination and other forms of conjuring in their practices. It is often believed that African indigenous paths disappeared with colonialism and Christian proselytization, but in fact, many continue to exist and have adapted and adopted elements from Christianity, Buddhism and Islam.

Afro-Brazilian

There is a unique and fascinating blend of the religious customs native to Brazil and those brought forward by slaves from Africa that has given birth to the indigenous path in Brazil. While according to Patheos.com (n.d.), some refer to these practices as "new religions", they are some of the oldest practices in the region. These religious practices meld and incorporate a wide variety and scope to include:

- a blend of African, Amerindian, and Catholic beliefs characterized by a great variety of spirits, African deities, saints (including Jesus and Mary), leaders, ancestors, and natural forces;
- the leaving of offerings including coins, liquor, flowers, candles, and food to spirits in public places;
- elaborate festivals and celebrations;
- an emphasis on spirit possession, divination, animal sacrifices, and ritual cult centers.

Afro-Caribbean

Like their counterparts in Afro-Brazilian practices, Indigenous Afro-Caribbean Religions are those that have combined beliefs and practices brought to the Caribbean by African slaves with the religious beliefs and practices native to the islands. Of these traditions, perhaps the best known is Voodoo commonly practiced in Haiti and the Dominican Republic. It is a blend of Roman Catholic rituals and theology and magical elements from various African traditions. Adherents acknowledge a supreme god, but also have many other highly venerated divinities called the Loa. The Loa include African gods, local leaders and deified ancestors, as well as Catholic saints. Patheos.com (n.d) shares that the priests and priestesses of Voodoo oversee a variety of rituals and ceremonies which include song, vigorous spirited dance, prayer, divination, healings, and animal sacrifice.

There are also other prominent indigenous Afro-Caribbean religions. One such is Rastafarianism, popular on the island of Jamaica among the black Jamaicans and centers on the worship on Haile Selassie I, former Emperor of Ethiopia (who is believed to be divine). As such Rastafarians believe blacks are the reincarnated Israelites whom God will eventually restore to Africa where they will be served by whites. The lifestyle often includes a vegetarian diet, dreadlock hair, and the smoking of ganja (marijuana).

Other Afro-Caribbean religions include Shango in Grenada and Trinidad, Santeria in Cuba, and the Convince and Cumina cults in Jamaica. All of these are derivations of the original formative blending of African traditions brought through the slave trade and native practices of the local islands. Many of these traditions migrated to mainland North America with the trading of slaves, particularly along the gulf coast and most significantly in Louisiana.

North America

Like most indigenous practices on other continents, the North American paths are a plethora of local traditions with variance in language, ritual practice, beliefs and customs. Further, Patheos.com (n.d.) contends that "as with other ancient traditions, the term "religion" is less than adequate in describing indigenous North American beliefs and rituals. More accurately labeled "worldviews," these traditions make no distinction between the religious and secular, or the natural and supernatural realms" (retrieved from http://www.patheos.com/Library/North-America.html)

"First Nations People" is the term preferred for referring to the indigenous in North America. The practices of the North American Indigenous are also animistic; as such the adherents share beliefs that not only connect individuals to each other as all of one spirit and sacred, but also to nature and the spirits. In essence all things are spiritual beings, including natural phenomena (e.g.; mountains, rivers, lakes, forests, stones, plants and herbs, clouds, etc.)

The traditions discern spiritual, social and political life. It includes the fulfilling of one's communal duties, and also the structure of authority which is often determined by age and the veneration of one's ancestors. It is difficult to make sweeping generalizations about the practices of the more than 300 individual communities and cultures. However what can be extrapolated is that most of these communities have rituals and ceremonies for the important rites of passage and celebrations: birth, puberty, death, harvest, hunting, etc. Like most indigenous practices, these traditions have mythologies, lessons and beliefs that are passed on orally.

South America

Like North America and other continents were there are indigenous paths, South America's indigenous are also as varied as the many languages and cultures in which they are embedded. Patheos.com (n.d.) posits that as these too were oral traditions, many have become extinct or have been altered since the introduction of European colonialists and evangelists on the continent (Retrieved from http://www.patheos.com/Library/South-America.html {n.d.}).

These traditions have creation myths describing the creation of the world and many spiritual beings active in the world. Accordingly, there are some South American traditions that believe in a supreme being who creates the world, while others believe the world came out of nothing. Some have persons of religious and spiritual authority such as priests, diviners, and shamans and there are many rituals within these traditions that center on the calendar and the stars.

Like most other indigenous religions there is an element of animism in which spirit and divinity is held in most objects, some holding more significance than others and these rituals can be related to the activities of spiritual beings as well as to other aspects of nature. Some traditions have initiation rites for men and women; these rituals help define the role of an individual within their community.

European Religions

The pre-Christian history of religion in Europe was and is perhaps the most difficult to ascertain. It was very diverse and very complex and like all indigenous paths, was varied by culture, language, tribe and affinity. With the rapid, extensive and frequent conquest on the continent, many traditions merged, were supplanted or otherwise extinguished. Before the introduction and spread of Christianity, each country had its own indigenous religious traditions. The 1st millennium B.C.E. saw the growth and spread of the Celts throughout Europe. It reached as far north as Britain by 450 B.C.E. and was followed by incursions by pre-Christian Germanic tribes such as the Angles, Saxons and Jutes during the first millennium C.E. Around 55 C.E. there was a Roman invasion of the Brits which in turn pushed the Celtic people to the Western edge, specifically to Ireland, Wales, Scotland, Cornwall, and Brittany. With their conquests, the Roman Empire spread pre-Christian religions such as Mithraism and the Imperial cult throughout Europe before also facilitating the proliferation of Early Christianity (Retrieved from http://www.philtar.ac.uk/encyclopedia/europe/geness.html {n.d.}).

The Ancient Celts

The Celtic religious festivals centered on the wheel of the year, fertility and harvests. The year was divided into two periods of six months signified by two major feasts. Beltaine (May 1) the "Fire of Bel", was the spring festival with a tradition that on that day the druids drove cattle between two fires as a protection against disease and maidens danced the maypole to welcome fertility of man and seed. Samhain (November 1) originally "summer," but later came to mark summer's end. These two six month periods were equally divided by the feasts of Imbolc (February 1) and Lughnasadh (August 1). Imbolc was a feast of purification for the farmers, sometimes called Oímelc ("sheep milk") as a reference to the lambing season or the feast of Brigid/Bride and Lughnasadh, the feast of the god Lugh also called Lammas and signifies the first harvest. (Retrieved from http://history-world.org/celts%20religious_beliefs_and_practices_.htm {n.d.})

Germanic Indigenous

For the purpose of this discussion ancient Germanic religion refers to a complex system of stories, lore, beliefs, and practices of and among the Germanic-speaking peoples before the indoctrination to Christianity. Like other indigenous faiths most of these religions were integrated into the Germanic daily life and culture and as such were influential in the formation of European civilization. It is believed that the origins of these practices date back several millennia before the 1st century B.C.E. with influence that extended from the Black Sea to Scandinavia and Greenland. The religions are based on the worship of a variety of gods, which are related not only to the cosmos, but also to nature. In addition to the gods, guardian spirits and dwarfs who were believed to have crafted the treasures of the gods, also held a role. Germanic rituals included animal sacrifice to the gods as well as festivals honoring the gods. The Sacred text was the *Prosse Edda* (Retrieved from http://www.patheos.com/Library/Germanic.html {n.d.}).

New Religions

Rubinstein (n.d.) asserts that new religious movement (NRM) is a term applied to all new faiths that have arisen worldwide over the past several centuries. Ofttimes it is used for what is sometimes called a cult; the latter being a pejorative connotation. NRM's have a number of shared characteristics and traits. They are often pluralistic, eclectic, and they freely combine practices from diverse sources within their respective belief systems. Further, Rubenstein (n.d.) suggests that while most contend ancient origins NRM's are by definition *new* in that they offer innovative religious experiences within the social and cultural modern world. Many are also regarded as *countercultural* by there adherents and others and are thought to be alternatives to the mainstream religions of Western society, particularly mainstream Christianity.

Generally, these NRMs emerged to address specific needs that many adherents cannot satisfy through more traditional religious organizations or modern secularism. Indeed many are the direct products of and responses to the scientific worldview, modern culture, and pluralism. Most are direct derivatives of other belief structures while some (Paganism and Wicca for instance) are reconstructionist in nature and in some rare instances, re-emergence of oral traditions and familial customs.

Baha'i

Momen (n.d.) contends that the Baha'i faith was founded in the mid-19th century C.E. in Iran by Siyyid 'Ali Mohammad, a Shi'ite Muslim, who proclaimed that he was "the Gate," (the Bab) a special interpreter of the Qur'an with unique insight and prophetic abilities, thus he was the *Hidden Imam*. One of his disciples, Mirza Hoseyn 'Ali Nuri, known as Baha'u'llah, spread the Bab's teachings which eventually evolved into the Baha'i faith, and it is Baha'u'llah who is most typically known as the founder of the tradition.

A key element of the belief that the Baha'i puts forth is that God is transcendent and unknowable to man; further that God's manifestation is understood in Baha'i to come not just through the Bab and Baha'u'llah, but also through the world's other religious prophets, including Abraham, Moses, Mohammed, Krishna, and the Buddha.

Christian Science

Officially the *Church of Christ, Scientist*, Christian Science is a religion that focuses on spiritual healing through prayer. A key formative premise is to restore the healing works of the early Christian church. It was founded in the late 19th century C.E. by Mary Baker Eddy. While there is some agreement in the Christian Science teachings and Protestant theology, there are also significant differences. Many of the teachings are based on the book by Eddy and her interpretations of biblical accounts of

Jesus' healings. (Retrieved from http://www.patheos.com/Library/Christian-Science.html {n.d.})

ISKCON (Hare Krishna)

Formally known as ISKCON, the International Society of Krishna Consciousness, the Hare Krishna movement is a semi-monastic religious movement based on Vaishnava Hinduism. Zeller (n.d.) posits that the Hare Krishna movement is in part modeled on the *bhakti* (loving devotion) movement of the 16th-century Hindu saint Caitanya. It was founded in 1965 C.E. by A.C. Bhaktivedanta, who moved to the United States from India with the intention of bringing "Krishna consciousness" to the West.

Jehovah's Witnesses

Davies-Stofka, Mulhern and Kinnard (n.d.) contend that the Jehovah's Witnesses was founded late 19th century C.E. in the United States. Its founder was Charles Taze Russell and grew out of the Christian Millerite. One of the key premises of the faith is that the Second Coming of Christ has already occurred (in a spiritual, invisible form) and the visible form that will follow will include the establishment of Christ's millennial kingdom here on earth. The name "Jehovah's Witnesses" came in 1931 under the leadership of Joseph Franklin Rutherford.

Jehovah's Witnesses adhere to only the *New World Translation Bible* as their sacred text.

There are major departures from traditional Christian teachings, including a rejection of the Trinity and most holidays and celebrations. Jehovah's Witnesses continue to engage in strong evangelistic missions programs as well as lifestyles based on a strict moral code of conduct. Adherents are expected to actively and aggressively engage in door-to-door proselytizing and evangelism which includes the distribution of books and the Watch Tower magazine as well as attending meetings at the Kingdom Hall which represents their places of worship.

Scientology

The Church of Scientology was founded by L. Ronald Hubbard in 1954 and according to Melton (n.d.) considers his teachings, including his popular book *Dianetics: The Modern Science of Mental Health*, as its essential texts. The faith espouses that the human mind is often restricted by its subconscious thoughts ("reactive mind") and needs to be freed from negative thoughts ("engrams") under the direction of a counselor (an "auditor") in order to release its everlasting spirit ("thetan"). As well, Melton (n.d.) contends that "once all of the engrams have been removed, the Scientologist is able to live spiritually free, a state called the *"Clear "*.

Unitarian-Universalism

The result of the 1961 merging of two, pluralistic, Christian-based religious movements, Unitarian-Universalism (commonly referred to as UU) emerged. While from Christian origins, many Unitarian-Universalists claim they are not a Christian denomination. Core Unitarianism originally organized during the 16th century C.E. reformation in Poland, Transylvania, and England, and then later developed from a break with the Protestant Puritans in New England. They reject the doctrine of the Triune nature of God and claim a singular unity of God.

After splitting from the Baptist and Congregationalist groups, the Universalists formed in the 18th century C.E. This spilt resulted from a disagreement over a teaching that claimed only a small number of people would be saved. Universalists believe and assert that God will restore all humanity and that eternal torment in hell is a fabrication not supported by the Bible.

Primarily in North America and the United States in particular these congregations are noted for their attention and participation in issues of social justice including equality in gender, sexual orientation and race.

Originally Unitarian-Universalists viewed the Bible as an authority however, there is currently much discourse regarding its authority and sacredness. While most Unitarian-Universalist congregations use ritual practices and hymns, a clear majority of their practices are based on experience and reason. There is a rejection of the use of confessions or creeds as well as relying on tradition or clerical authority. Thus there is a belief in the freedom of religious thought and tolerance regarding differing rituals and customs in worship and religious practice.

New Age

Zeller (n.d.) shares that the term "*New Age* is an umbrella term used to describe an organization of diverse groups that share an enthusiasm for the creation of a new era (or "New Age") exemplified by harmony and enlightenment." As such he contends that there are no distinct boundaries within the New Age community and many unifying themes. Perhaps first is that the arrival of the New Age will initiate a heightened spiritual consciousness which will be accompanied by social and personal transformation. This transformation will permit the eradication of all social and ecological ills, including hunger, sickness, poverty, racism, sexism, and war. Further another theme is that individuals can access and sample this enlightenment through personal spiritual transformation, healing, and growth.

The movement was most popular during the 1970s and 1980s through the teachings of David Spangler and other metaphysical religious groups and continues in popularity today. Historically, there has been some form of this movement since the 2nd century C.E. beginning with

Gnosticism. Other forms of practice include Rosicrucianism, Freemasonary, and the teachings of Helena Blavatsky.

Most New Age practices ascribe to a variety of natural healing practices and traditional medicines including herbal therapy, acupressure, acupuncture, natural foods, and spiritual healings. There is no standard doctrine within the New Age Movement; however there is a unifying factor in that many teachings focus on individual autonomy, relativism, enlightenment, and spiritualism.

Paganism (Neo-paganism)

McColman (n.d.) informs us that paganism, as a path, is an amalgam of a wide variety of traditions with a reverence for and an emphasis on nature. It should be noted that most *pre-Christian* faiths and religions were considered "pagan" according to Contemporary Christian teachings. For the purpose of this study *pagan* shall refer to the neo-pagan paths of recent order.

Most pagan traditions are animistic and focus on a revival of ancient polytheistic religious practices. Paganism does not profess traditional religion *per se* because it does not have any official doctrine, but it does have some common characteristics shared amongst the traditions. Further, many pagan groups now stand as temples or churches with organized "congregations" or covens as some prefer to be called and recognition in their local communities. Within Paganism, monotheism is generally not accepted though many traditions hold that the God and Goddess (hence masculine and feminine forms) are but aspects a single divine being. For most in this faith, there is a particular interest in the revival of ancient polytheist traditions including the Norse and Celtic (Britain) traditions.

While some pagan traditions can trace roots to 19th century C.E. European nationalism (including the British Order of Druids), according to McColman (n.d.) most are rooted in the 1960s and emphasize a spiritual interest in nature as well as archetypal psychology. Adler (2006), infers that alongside the resurgence of *occult*, *magickal* and *New Age* groups, there has been a parallel growth of the diverse and decentralized pagan movement. Often, Adler (2006) shares, pagan groups are misunderstood and unnoticed. She further notes that most pagans are individualist, eclectic and fiercely autonomous, thus drawing an even more stark contrast to *traditional* religions and for that matter the *cults* previously referred to in the discussion of the New Religious Movements.

One of the most common beliefs is in the divine presence in nature and a reverence of the natural order in life. As many are based on Celtic indigenous practices, there is typically deference to the Celtic wheel of the year and thus ones spiritual growth and development is related to the cycles of the Earth. Often there is a great emphasis placed on ecological concerns. In addition to holding sacred and a celebration of Nature, many pagans also worship a host of gods and goddesses, including spirits and spirit forms as well as deceased family members. In this sense, many pagans try to honor their ancestry and ancestors. Some pagans, but not all, include ritual magic and high celebrations. Finally, McColman (n.d.) suggests most pagan traditions are intentionally reconstructionist and they aim to revive the lost rituals of the indigenous and ancient traditions of many peoples.

Wicca

Wicca is a one of many of the recently reconstructed neo-pagan religions based in part on elements of ancient, pre-Christian Celtic indigenous religion. In this sense it is both a very new and a very ancient religion. In fact, there are some traditions within Wicca that draw both lineage and belief from longstanding family customs and oral teachings. Wiccan traditions form the single largest religion within the neo-paganism paths.

Like the many derivations within other spiritual paths (Christianity for instance) there are many traditions within Wicca. Each tradition has its own unique practices, rituals, teachings and beliefs. All share in common recognition of the God and Goddess. Also in common is a respect for masculine and feminine equally with recognition of a divine presence of both. There is also a profound respect and veneration of nature. (Retrieved from http://www.religioustolerance.org/wic_term.htm)

There are no sacred text *per se* in Wicca, however, most traditions have a book of rituals, spelles, allspices and teachings (sometimes referred to as a *Book of Shadows*) that is shared and transmitted as a part of the learning for adherents. The *Foxwood Book of Laws* articulates the primary principles which are shared by most if not all Wiccan Traditions: The "Three-fold Law" and the "Wiccan Rede". The Rede states in essence: one can do whatever one wants, as long as it harms no one, including oneself (this also includes creatures and creations in nature).

The Three-fold Law likewise states that the good one does to another returns, magnified three times and any harm also returns threefold. ReligiousTolerence.org says it best: "This heavily motivates Wiccans to behave ethically and to avoid harming others".

ReligiousTolerence.org also offers the following passage which is of significance in understanding the oft-stated misunderstanding of Wicca and Paganism:

> "Historically, Wicca has been incorrectly associated with Satanism. The roots of this confusion can be traced back to Europe during the Witch burning times of the late Middle Ages and Renaissance. Witches were accused of worshipping Satan and selling their soul to him. This false belief continues today, and is still being actively promoted by some Christian individuals and ministries. Some conservative Christians believe in

the literal truth of some Biblical passages which say that the gods and goddesses that are worshiped by non-Christians are really Satan or one of his demons. They define all non-Christian religions as forms of Satanism. In reality, Wicca is unrelated to Satanism or to black magic. Their governing principles, rules of behavior, basic beliefs about deity, humanity and the rest of the universe, system of morality, etc. are quite different -- often opposite. The main Wiccan symbol is the upright 5 pointed star (called a pentagram), and a pentagram within a circle, (called a pentacle). One point of the star is generally aligned upwards, except when it refers to the second degree initiation or male principle. Satanists inverted both symbols and adopted them as their own symbol."

ReligiousTolerance.org also shares that many Wiccans assert the word "*witch*" as a synonym for "*Wiccan*" and others have abandoned the term witch being of the belief that centuries of religious propaganda have rendered very negative connotations that cannot possibly be salvaged. Conversely, there is a belief among some Wiccans that to abandon the word is to defame and discredit the memories of the tens of thousands of innocents, witches and other heretics who were accused of "Witchcraft," and were individually tortured and executed during the Christian "*Burning Times,*" circa 1450 to 1792 C.E. also known as the Inquisition. A powerful statement by ReligiousTolerence.org regarding this matter is such: "We advocate that the word be carefully pre-defined before it is used in a speech or article that may be read by the general public. Even then, the word will still be filtered through the reader's or listener's belief systems. The latter may well have been influenced by centuries of Christian propaganda and decades of horror movies."

Figure 1 Historical Timeline of Religions

Faith, Society and the Individual

Should each person live the ideals propounded by the founders of his religion, unaffected by greed or hate, then the world will be a happy and peaceful habitation for man... Man can realize his mission on the earth only when he knows himself as Divine and when he reveres all others as Divine

~ Sri Sathaya Sai Baba, unk

Religion the Social Institution

Roberts and Yamane (2012), proffer that religion represents an interdependent system by which segments of society and communities achieve a bond. This bonding occurs by a shared meaning -- that being faith, a world view or ethos, a set of beliefs or mythology, rituals and system of symbols—thus a symbolic interaction between members, a sense of belonging to a group (reference group), a system of directive ethics or values and finally a set of routine social expectations and patterned behaviors.

In this regard, sociological theory holds that religion represents one of the seven pillars of institutions of society. In this, reference is not made to particular paths of faith or organized "churches", but rather the very foundations by which all societies are crafted, supported and sustained. With the other social institutions—politics, education, family, economy or exchange, and the newer pillars media and health/healthcare – religion forms the core of all societies. That is not to say that all members of a given society are religious, but all societies have some means for its members (who so choose) to understand and appreciate that which cannot be explained or to connect to that which is profound and divine.

Dictionary.com shares the following definition for religion: "a set of beliefs concerning the cause, nature, and purpose of the universe, especially when considered as the creation of a superhuman agency or agencies, usually involving devotional and ritual observances, and often containing a moral code governing the conduct of human affairs -- a specific fundamental set of beliefs and practices generally agreed upon by a number of persons or sects" (Retrieved from http://dictionary.reference.com/browse/religion).

To fully understand religion and its impact and value to society, we must understand the definition and nature of systems. To be sure, a system is an organized whole made up of components that interact in a way distinct from their interaction with other entities and which endures over some period of time. Further defined, a system is a set of interrelated elements that interact dynamically with each other and the environment and have identifiable properties.

These definitions are based on the theories and preponderances of Ludwig Von Bertalanffy's open systems model (circa 1962). An open system (Figure 2) is any distinct entity -- a cell, a person, a forest, or, in this instance, a society or segment of society like a religion -- that takes in resources from its environment, processes them in some way, and produces output.

To survive, such a system depends on its environment and on interactions between its component parts, elements or subsystems. Thus when taking an open-systems approach, we must look both inward and outward at the system and the environment in which it exists. Finally, we examine such because we are interested in relationships and patterns of interaction between subsystems, components and their environments within a society.

So why is the systems model appropriate for this discussion of religion? Simple really, to undestand religion, one must understand its place of significance in society and in the development and evolution of humans in society. For each religion holds significance to a segment of society and forms the basis of many of the beliefs, culture, ethics, laws and order of that society. There is a finite interrelationship and interdependence between society and the religions within that society. Each is a major component and susbsystem of the other, each proving vital to the existence of the other.

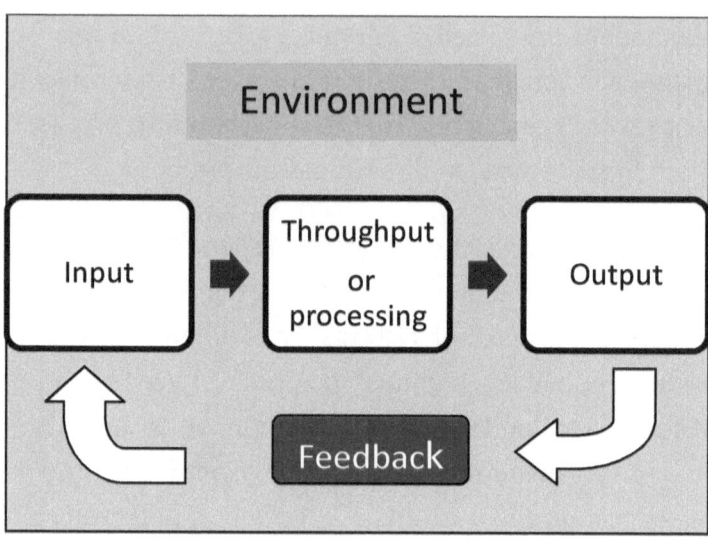

Figure2 The Open Systems Model

There is an irony to the study of religion through the sociological lense, and that rests in the notion that the acknowledged "fathers" of sociology, all in their own way, pondered and expressed an immenient demise of religion with the advent of the sociological approach and school of thought. But to the contrary, religion has survived and in many ways thrived with the advents of modern sciences, both psychology and sociology respectively. In many ways, the role of religion has given rise to many studies and examinations and as a result we understand better the significance religion plays in virtually all aspects of society and human existance. This view to the importance of religion in and on society lends to a discussion of major schools of sociological perspective.

First, structural-functionalism. This perspective contends that there is a structure and a function to all aspects of a society. Based on the works of Auguste Comte, E`mile Durkhein, Herbert Spencer, Talcott Parson and Robert Merton amongst others, this framework gives us a view to understand how societies are structured and thus what function the various sub-systems and structure within a society hold. Religion, then, being one of the pillars of social structure holds a place of prominence. A society would not function or would cease to function without this important subsystem and its associated components.

This relationship, Roberts and Yamane (2012) explains is multidimensional and extremely complex. Religion, in this context, is viewed as one of the cultural universals. Indeed, as stated in the previous section, religions exist and have existed before man began to record and document experience. One of the simplest examples offered by Roberts and Yamane (2012) holds that religion allows one to feel and experience a source of power and hope that is greater than one's own available resources.

Another perspective is that of conflict theory. Karl Marx is considered the father of conflict theory and is often misquoted as saying "religion is the opiate of the masses" Actually the paraprhase is a poor translation of original German phrase *"Die Religion ... ist das Opium des*

Volkes", and that interpretation is slightly out of context from the original full text translation which follows:

> "The foundation of irreligious criticism is: Man makes religion, religion does not make man. Religion is, indeed, the self-consciousness and self-esteem of man who has either not yet won through to himself, or has already lost himself again. But man is no abstract being squatting outside the world. Man is the world of man – state, society. This state and this society produce religion, which is an inverted consciousness of the world, because they are an inverted world. Religion is the general theory of this world, its encyclopaedic compendium, its logic in popular form, its spiritual point d'honneur, its enthusiasm, its moral sanction, its solemn complement, and its universal basis of consolation and justification. It is the fantastic realization of the human essence since the human essence has not acquired any true reality. The struggle against religion is, therefore, indirectly the struggle against that world whose spiritual aroma is religion...Religious suffering is, at one and the same time, the expression of real suffering and a protest against real suffering. Religion is the sigh of the oppressed creature, the heart of a heartless world, and the soul of soulless conditions. It is the opium of the people...The abolition of religion as the illusory happiness of the people is the demand for their real happiness. To call on them to give up their illusions about their condition is to call on them to give up a condition that requires illusions. The criticism of religion is, therefore, in embryo,

the criticism of that vale of tears of which religion is the halo"

(Retrieved from http://en.wikipedia.org/wiki/Opium_of_the_people)

The notion of conflict then is inherent in our understanding of religion. In part because there have been countless conflicts between religions (hence the term "blood religions" attributed to the Abrahamic faiths) and countless conflicts *due to* religions. Conflict theory contends that there are struggles between disparate segments of society. In the view of Marx, that struggle is between the classes, those with wealth and those without. It goes to reason then that he (Marx) would have issue with the wealth that was accumulated by the church historically. The conflict sociological perspective doesn't just examine how social structures help society to operate, but instead looks at how social patterns can *cause* some people in society to be dominant while others are oppressed.

We can take our understanding of conflict theory even further. Marxian theory suggests that conflict manifests in all aspects of human life. There have been interreligious conflicts as alluded to previously and there have been intrafaith conflict as in the historic separations and epic battles of Protestant and Catholic believers in the Christian faith. A further application of conflict theory would be in understanding conflict between religious and secular authority. Roberts and Yamane (2012) contend that religion can prove contentious in determining or recognizing proper authority. In this instance, a religious value structure may come in direct conflict with secular values or even laws. There are numerous contemporary examples of this concept, many playing out on the political arena in the United States. Abortion, euthanasia, death penalties, recognition of same gender marriages or relationships, even the religion of elected officials or candidates are all clear exemplars of this issue.

There have also been numerous cases world wide where there has been conflicts with deeply held traditions: polygamy, male and/or female circumcision, the refusal of recognized western medicinal techniques, or something as seemingly simple as Amish children being required to attend school beyond a certain age are all examples of these inherant conflicts between religious values or laws and secular values or laws.

Of course we can always look to the conflcit between good and evil, right and wrong, moral and amoral. These can be either inter- or intra-personal in nature but none-the-less pose significant strain and distress on individuals and societies as they struggle to reconcile. As a broad concept, conflict theory draws our attention to power differentials such as gender, class, religion and race conflict, and contrast historically dominant ideologies, faiths and beliefs. It is, as such, a macro level analysis of society that sees society as an arena of inequality that generates conflict and often through conflict, social change. But this can also have a profound impact in the micro level religious discourse.

The final sociological school of thought that will be examined here is that of symbolic interactionism. This theoretical construct was purposed by such theorist as Max Weber and George Herbert Mead. Symbolic interactionism places emphasis on micro level social interactions that provide subjective meaning to human behavior.

The theory has a focus on the framework by which we can understand society as the product of the everyday interactions of individuals. From this we can assert that society is nothing more than the shared reality that people construct as they interact with one another. In many ways, this theory perhaps best explains from a scientific analysis the experience and importance of religion within society.

Herbert Blumer (1969), coined the term "symbolic interactionism," and offers three basic premises to the perspective:

1. Humans act toward things on the basis of the meanings they ascribe to those things.
2. The meaning of such things is derived from, or arises out of, the social interaction that one has with others and the society.

3. These meanings are handled in, and modified through, an interpretative process used by the person in dealing with the things he/she encounters.

With this perspective we can best appreciate religious significance. We can, as alluded to by Roberts and Yamane (2012), look to the complexity of the relationships among the components and subsytems of religious belief. Thus in our attempts to intergrate and understand those elements as the cohesive systems they represent, we must appreciate the following:

1. The symbols used by religions, which include rituals, mythology, deity, artifacts, and texts both encapsulates and defines the worldview and the ethos of a people. As such, these symbols garner powerful emotions and by shear repetition, reinforce one's worldview.
2. Ritual and mythology are generally mutually reinforcing mechanisms of a religious and symbolic system
3. One's worldview and ethos are themselves mutually reinforcing
4. And finally, all of these elements together provide a undeniable basis for a society's values.

We mustn't negate however that in a strict interpretation of symbolic interactionism, religion itself *is* a symbol. But as a theory (symbolic interactionism) with a focus on the micro level, that being on interaction of individuals in one another's presence, religion is and must be divided into many subsystems of smaller symbols. The deity, (God, gods, goddess{es}) are usually symbols of ultimate authority. Deities are viewed as creators of the universe (or world), and therefore they have the right to rule, to dictate behavior, and to reward those in the afterlife who behave properly.

Other symbols have included "paying" the Deity for blessings, whether that was sacrificing of ritual animals or even human beings or material donations. This could include tithing or conducting one's life as Deity expects or require up to devoting the whole life to the Deity as a priest or a monk, a nun or priestess, or even eunuchs. To further appreciate this reciprocity of subsystems, Figure 3 illustrates the interdependence of the components of religion.

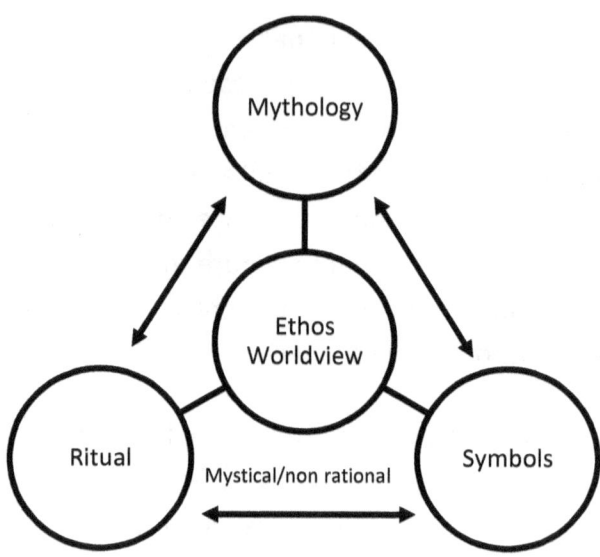

Figure 3 The interdependence of belief structures

Figure 4 offers a graphic depiction of man and religion and the components that compose our faith, beliefs, customs, traditions, teachings or texts and rituals.

Figure 4 Man and Religion

Man and Religion

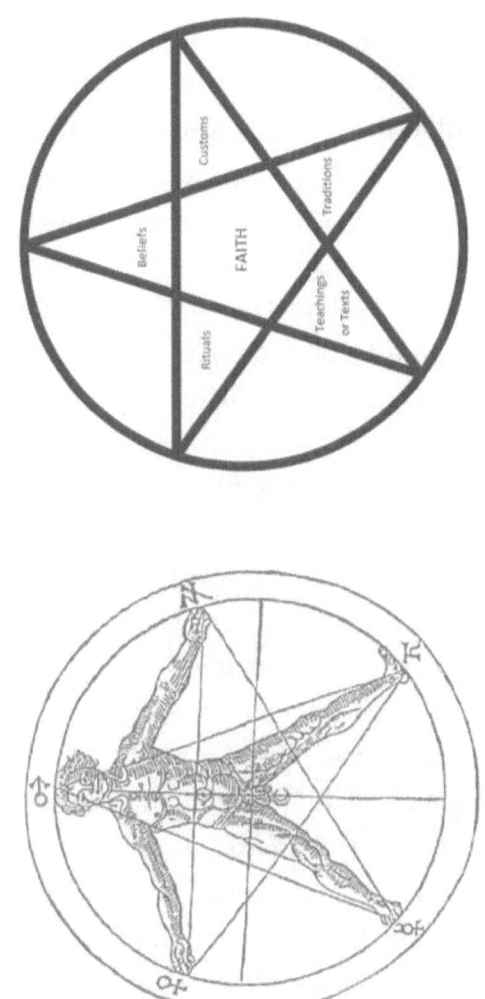

Religion: the Pillar

Demarest (2009) offers the following perspective on the journey to one's path or faith, "We enjoy journeying to pleasant places—to a magnificent national park, peaceful seashore or romantic overseas destination. We delight in the planning, the travel, the arrival and the stay itself, which together form the fabric of our exciting journey. Travel to interesting places renews and refreshes body and soul". (p 11) While it is true that not everyone is spiritual or on a religious path, the sheer number of adherents to religions and faith paths demonstrate the power and significance religions hold in societal order. To truly appreciate the significance religion plays in societies, an examination of the number of adherents to various paths and faiths is in order. Our first look will be to the number of adherents worldwide to the major paths articulated in the section on history. To advance statistical comparison, the numbers of non-religious, agnostic, atheist and secular persons are also included. For the purpose of this study the size or number (both worldwide and domestic) will refer to the number of people that subscribe to particular faiths as reported through organizational reports, census data for those countries that collect religious information as such, various polls and surveys, field work and finally estimates based on other forms of indirect data collections. Numbers presented are rounded and approximate estimates for statistical analysis only and do not reflect an "actual count" which would be difficult at best to ascertain.

Christianity in its many forms by far represents the largest single grouping of adherents with some 2.1 billion estimated worldwide. Islam (all branches) has some 1.5 billion followers. While we have focused discussions on the major "religions" we cannot overlook the "non-religious" or those that profess no path or faith. The secular, agnostic, atheist and non-religious represent some 1.1 billion. There are an estimated 900 million Hindus and 394 million who follow the teaching of Chinese traditional. Buddhist adherents number around 376 million while those that hold Indigenous faiths (in this purpose, indigenous worldwide include those of African origin or Diasporic) number near 401 million. Sikhism represents some 23 million and Judaism ranks with 14 million.

Baha'i has nearly 7 million followers worldwide and Jainism and Shinto both hold some 4 million to 4.2 million believers. Finally, Zoroastrianism has 2.6 million adherents and Neo-Pagans/Wiccans share approximately 1 million. Unitarian-Universalist and Scientology claim 800 thousand and 500 thousand followers respectively. Figure 5 presents a graphic depiction of these numbers.

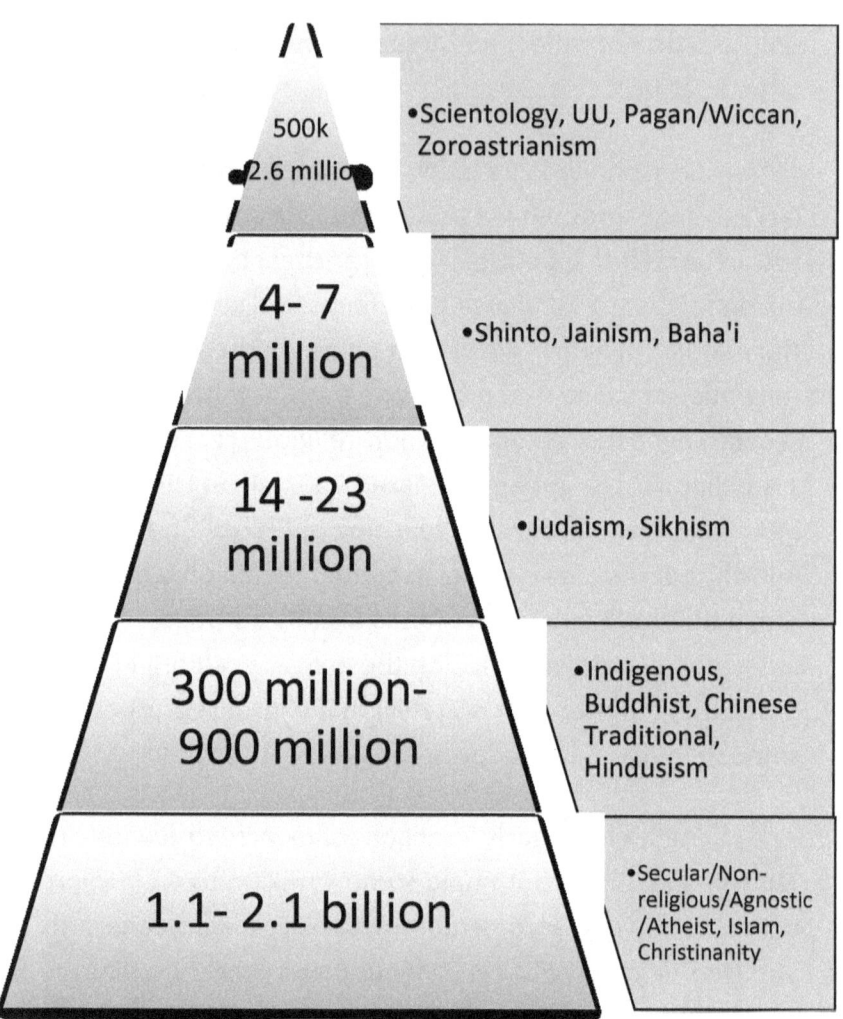

Figure5 Relative Comparison of Adherents

By contrast to "world" religions, the top 10 American religions and secular, non-religious, atheists and agnostics counted for statistical comparison, follows. These figures in Table 1 are based on the most recent collected data regarding religious belief and census calculations in 2004.

Table 1 Number of US Adherents

Religious Adherent Distribution United States of America

Religion (category)	Estimated adult adherents 2004
Christianity	224,437,959
Secular, Non-religious, Agnostic, Atheist	41,537,182
Judaism	3,995,371
Islam	1,558,068
Buddhism	1,527,019
Hinduism	1,081,051
Unitarian Universalist	887,703
Wiccan/Pagan	433,267
Indigenous (1st Americans)	145,363
Baha'i	118,549

Figure 6 gives a graphic representation of the distribution of religious adherents and non-adherents in the US. These numbers are in comparison to the US population of 293,655,404 adults for the same period. All data herein was retrieved from www.adherents.com.

Comparison numbers from a similar census taken years before reflect a significant shift in the number of adherents. While some religions saw significant declines, others saw growth; the numbers of secular, non-religious, atheist and agnostics have grown the most.

Figure6 Distribution of U.S. Religious Adherents

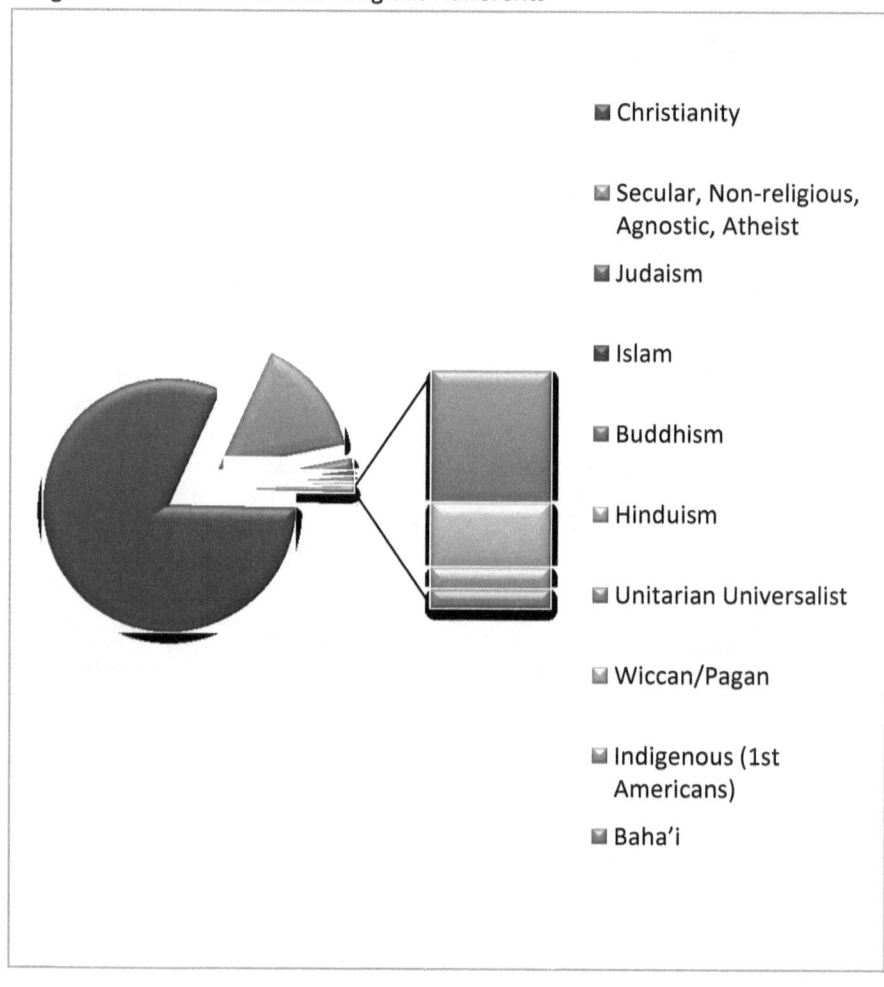

The Pew Forum (2009) discovered that Americans have a tendency to change religious affiliation early and often in their adulthood. The study reflects that about half of American adults changed religious affiliation at least once in their lifetimes with most leaving their childhood religion by age 24. This study further reflects that two thirds of former Catholics have become unaffiliated. As an example of some of the reasons for leaving, half of former Protestants that left say they left because they stopped believing in the Protestant teachings.

Perhaps most significantly, the Pew study revealed that many people left their religions because religions focus too much on rules, that the leaders are overly focused on power or greed, or because they think of religious people as insincere, judgmental and/or hypocritical. One finding shows that 71% of the Catholics that left that faith for a Protestant faith left because they felt their spiritual needs were not being met; the same finding held true for one half of all Protestants that left their "childhood" religion. In addition, there were a number that left because of church scandal or other disingenuous activity in their former faith.

Gender, Race and Age Differences

The sheer numbers of adherents to various religions, and the importance that religion holds in society leaves one to question if there are differences in religious practices and preferences based on gender, race or other strata. Flere (2007) contends that "it is generally acknowledged that women are more religious than men." Flere (2007) goes on to report that while data does indicate an increased religiosity amongst women when compared to men, there is not sufficient empirical data to validate this finding or to render more specificity. Further, what was found tends to be attributed to differential socialization, which is an extension of the well documented gender differences in socialization patterns, standards, and expectations.

Taylor, Chatters, Jayakody and Levin (1996), submit that there is a presence of consistent racial differences in religious involvement. Their study focused on "black and white" racial differences in religious involvement. Accordingly, as compared to whites, black respondents demonstrated higher levels of religious attendance (public acknowledgement) and private observations, i.e.; reading sacred texts or religious material. Taylor et al. (1996), also found that blacks were more likely to endorse a higher level of positive statements or sentiments towards their religion or faith. This study contends that the race disparities in involvement could be a result of the underlying distinction in the differentiation of religious and secular functions.

There are well recorded features in the black culture in America that give rise to a unique relationship with religious faith. Taylor et al. (1996) offer the following insight, "Black churches have actively sought to redress the social and political conditions which impact the lives of black Americans. The interdependence of secular and religious spheres was manifested in the role that religious institutions fulfilled in the development of educational institutions, social welfare efforts, civic and business concerns, as well as their involvement in social and political concerns."

Perhaps the most notable example of this relationship is the civil rights movement. There is perhaps an irony in that in many instances in modern times, the black church has used its influence to hinder the civil rights of others, namely gay and lesbian citizens. The preponderance of black pastors actively and vocally resisting the approval of civil marriage for same gender couples is an example of this irony.

Another interesting contrast along the demographic stratification is the difference in religious beliefs among the various generations acknowledged in American society. The Pew Forum on Religion and Public Life (2010) studied Religion among the Millennials. This study showed that young Americans born between 1980 and 2000 (18 to 29 year olds at the time of this study) were considerably less religious than previous generations. By comparison at similar ages, 26% of the Millennials were unaffiliated with an organized religion while with Gen X (snap shot = late 1990s) 20% were unaffiliated. For the Baby Boomer generation, the largest in America (snap shot = late 1970s), 13% when young adults were unaffiliated by comparison to the Millennials which were twice as unlikely to be affiliated.

Figure 7 reflects an analysis of the comparison when generations were at a similar age for the 5 living generations in America. For the oldest two generations, the comparison snapshot at the 1970's as no data exists on that population before the advent of similar studies in the early 1970s.

Figure7 Comparison of Religiously Unaffiliated by Generation

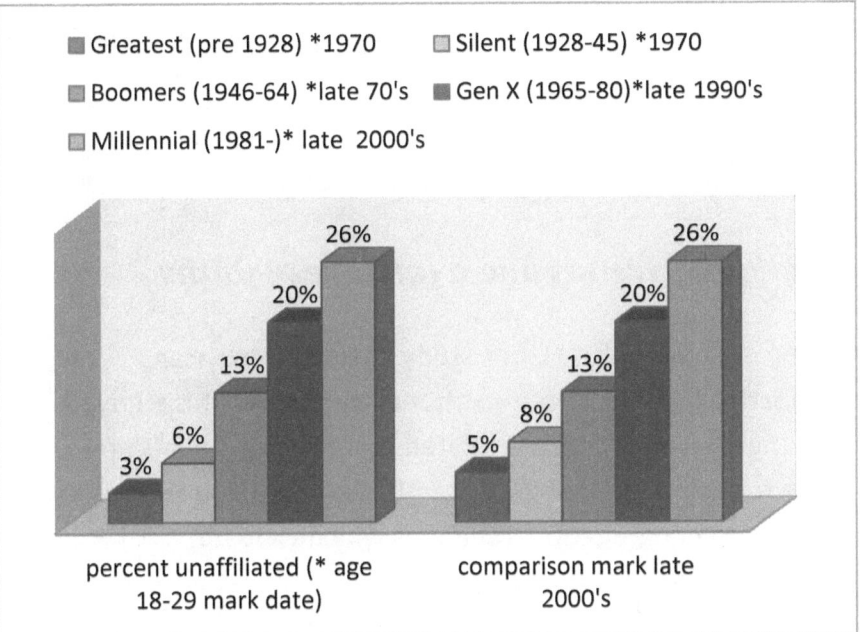

This data also revealed that as compared with older generations, fewer young Americans considered religion as very important in their lives. Still the youngest generation measured held fairly traditional practices and beliefs; many believe in some form of afterlife, the existence of heaven and hell and in miracles, all of which are shared by the older generations. This generation however noted praying less often then the elders. There are other noted differences in political and social opinions in that Millennials are:

- More accepting of homosexuality
- More accepting of legal abortion

- More inclined to view evolution as best to explain human life
- Less prone to see Hollywood and the Media as threats to morality
- Less likely to view the Bible (for Christian adherents) as the literal word of God

Religious trends and a mixture of faiths

Chaves (2011), in a study of North American Christians, offers 13 observational trends. For this study, 8 of the 13 trends that are related to individual beliefs are the focus. The remaining 5 trends identified, are related to Christian congregational changes which yield no significance to this analysis:

- Increasing religious diversity
    - The most dramatic change has been the number of Americans who claim no religious affiliation.
    - The increase in no religious affiliation has impacted the Protestant branch of Christianity more than others.
    - The number of Hindus, Buddhists and Muslims remain relatively small but is increasing exponentially with immigration.
    - The number of individuals claiming other than Judeo-Christian faith has more than doubled since the 1970s.

- - Americans have become more accepting of religious diversity and have grown to appreciate religions other than one's own. {Editorial note—the events of September 2001 have had a slight impact on the acceptance measures.}
- Fewer liberal Protestants
  - For Protestants there has been a continual shift from liberal and centrist mainline denominations to more conservative, evangelical and, in some cases, extreme denominations. It should be noted that this shift is more reflective of a decline of adherents of mainline (nee liberal) denominations and *not* an increase in evangelicals. Chaves (2011) gives a slight nod to suggest that upward social mobility has some impact on this trend. A look to recent political rhetoric and discourse and the use of social wedge issues has created even more polarization along the liberal/conservative spectrum as well as amongst the secular and religious spectrums.

- Softening involvement in religious congregations
    - There has been a steady and marked decline in attendance at "Sunday" services from the 1950s. This holds in contemporary findings as well.
- Declining belief in an inerrant Bible
    - In the last 30 years the number of individuals who profess that they believe the Bible should be taken literally has declined from approximately 40% to a little over 30%. As suggested by Chaves (2011), this might be a trend in connection with the increase in religious diversity tolerance which implies a declining confidence in a "special status" of one's own belief.
- Declining confidence in leaders of organized religion
    - There has been 10% drop in the number of Christians who have confidence in the leaders of their religion. There is corollary decrease in the confidence in leaders in general, but this trend is also reflected in the number of individuals who have an interest in a career in religious leadership.
- Tighter connection between religiosity and political conservatism
    - Chaves (2011) shares that there has been a tightening connection between political and social conservatism and Christian religiosity.

Further, these analyses also relate the frequency of church attendance on the opinions one holds regarding social issues. Chaves notes that "all and all, it is difficult to avoid the conclusions that the attitudinal distance between the most and least religiously active people in the U.S. society has increase in recent decades". (p.125) Chaves (2011) suggests that the attitudinal differences do not warrant the title "cultural wars", but anecdotal information and other data regarding the nature of religion and diversity of religion in the U.S. might suggest that from the eyes of a Christian, there is indeed a "battle" over culture and values. From the perspective of non-Christians, this trend might be indicative of the further diversification of faith.

- More disapproval of religions leader's political involvement
    - While we are seeing an increase in the connection between political conservatism and religiosity, the number of respondents that strongly agree that religious leaders should _not_ be involved in political debate or elections has increased steadily from 30% in 1991 to 44% in 2008. Additionally, the number of respondents that believed

that religious leaders should *not* try to influence government decisions also increased from 22% in 1991 to 38% in 2008.
- Finally, an increasingly diffuse spirituality

The trend and phenomenon in America referred to, as Chaves (2011) puts it, being "spiritual but not religious" is well know but , Chaves contends this should not be exaggerated. Data in this study reflects that 80% describe themselves as both spiritual and religious. Conversely, this study reveals that non religious people are more likely to say they are *spiritual* and the trend is more prominent amongst younger individuals. In fact, one in five under forty describes themselves as spiritual and not religious compared to one in ten in 1998. This same data reflects that an increasing number of people who espouse spiritual inclinations that do not lead them to become involved in "conventional religious organizations"

The same analysis reveals that there has been an increase in the number of individuals that believe is some form of afterlife or life after death and likewise there has been what Chaves (2011) terms a "small but noticeable" increase in a "generic and diffuse spirituality".

The Great Faith Mixing Bowl

We have examined the significant role religion and faith plays in society, the differences amongst the number of adherents, the differences along some lines of social stratification and trends in religions, particular to the largest faith path but extractable to many others. What remains to help shape the understanding of faith society and the individual is to explore how many in America mix multiple faiths to form their personal path and spiritual connections.

The Pew Forum study entitled Many Americans Mix Multiple Faiths (2009), shares a very intriguing perspective, "The religious beliefs and practices of Americans do not fit neatly into conventional categories". (p 2) This study of 4013 survey respondents purports that 35% say they regularly attend religious services at more than one place or occasionally attend religious services at more than one place (26%) and that most of these respondents (24% of the public overall) indicate that they sometimes attend religious services of a faith different from their own. Further this study shows that among those who report attending religious services at least once a week, 39% (representing 4 in 10 Americans) say they attend services at multiple places and approximately 28% (3 in 10 Americans) go to services outside their own faith. Contributing to this finding is the number of Americans in mixed or multi religious marriages which is common.

While Christianity remains the single largest group of adherents as demonstrated previously in Figure 6, there are significant minority groups of other faiths with an affirmation of belief in a variety of Eastern or New Age beliefs. Some examples are as follows:

- 23% of Christians (25% of the public overall) believe in and follow some form of astrology.
- 22% of Christians (24% of the public overall) say they believe in reincarnation, the notion of being reborn in this world multiple times.
- 15% of respondents have consulted a fortuneteller or a psychic.
- Almost one-in-five share that they have seen or been in the presence of ghosts.
- Nearly three-in-ten Americans say they have felt in touch with someone who has already died.
- 49% (nearly half) of the public says they have had a religious or mystical experience, which for the Pew Study was defined as a "moment of sudden religious insight or awakening".
- Finally, religious and mystical experiences were more common today among 30% of those who are unaffiliated.

Further findings from the Pew Study lend an even greater appreciation of the mix of religious beliefs, at least in the American culture. A quarter of adults express belief in tenets of certain Eastern religions with 24% believing in reincarnation and 23% believing in yoga not just as exercise but as a spiritual practice. Likewise similar numbers share belief in elements of New Age spirituality, with 26% expressing belief in some form of animism (that is again spiritual energy located in physical things such as mountains, trees or crystals and the like). There were fewer people (16%) who believed in the "evil eye" or that individuals can cast spells that cause bad things to happen to someone. Notably missing was a comparison in the Pew Study of those who believe in healing spelles or prayers.

A report released by Brown (2007), however, contends that there is a new look at the significance of such practices sharing that the traditional barriers between the notion of spiritual and medical healing are coming down. This article shares that more than 80% of Americans said they believe that God or other divinity supernaturally heals people in answer to prayer (or spells). Some of the other practices that in addition to Christian prayer for divine healing, have gained scientific merit are rooted in Eastern and Indigenous alternative healing practices sourced in metaphysical spiritualities practices such as yoga, reiki, chiropractic and Therapeutic Touch acupuncture, homeopathy the use of sweat lodges and "energy work".

Brown (2007) also contends that an increasing numbers of medical schools now include and encourage courses on patient spirituality. In other forms, clinical studies of the effectiveness of intercessory prayer and practice have increased in recent years. There is even a growing body of scientific evidence and legal standing for the use of the here-to-fore maligned use of marijuana as natural herbal for relieving chronic pain, glaucoma, and in the treatment of cancer and HIV/AIDS patients. This is but one example of the integration of "alternative" and spiritual practices with merit in the body of knowledge regarding health and healing. (Retrieved from http://newsinfo.iu.edu/web/page/normal/4779.html)

A further look at the Pew Forum study (2009) reveals that generally three in ten Americans or 29% say they have felt in touch with someone who has passed away, with almost 18% of respondents, which represents one out of five Americans say they have been near or experienced a ghost, while another 15% say they have consulted a psychic, diviner or fortuneteller.

In summation, the Pew Study contends that 65% (or six in ten) American adults hold some belief in or report having experience with at least one of these diverse supernatural phenomena:

- belief in astrology
- consulting a psychic
- belief in animism or spiritual energy located in physical things
- belief in yoga as spiritual practice
- belief in the "evil eye"
- belief in reincarnation
- having been in touch with the dead
- experiencing a ghostly encounter

As previously revealed by Brown (2007), 80% of Americans believe in some form of prayerful, holistic or spiritual healing.

In our look to compare along the social strata we find, based on the Pew Forum Study (2009), that mystical or religious experiences tend to be most common among people who attend religious services regularly and, compared with other religious traditions, white evangelical Protestants (men in particular) consistently express lower levels of acceptance of both New Age beliefs (spiritual energy in physical things and astrology) or Eastern beliefs (reincarnation, yoga and the like) and Blacks are much more likely than Whites or Hispanics (69%, 47% and 44%, respectively) to report religious or mystical experiences.

Finally over 55% of baby boomers (age 50-64) identify with such experiences, in contrast to fewer millennials and greatest/silent generation seniors (43% each). All of these findings shape an interesting mosaic for a look to areas of faith and belief in which all faiths share commonality. For as shown with the increased diversification of religious practice, the shift in adherents, the mixing of sometimes multiple faith practices and trends affecting paths, it is clear that we must develop a deeper and greater appreciation for those elements of faith, spirituality, religion, and frankly humanity that we all share.

Understanding Belief and Religious Faith Convergences

NAMASTE "I honor the place in you where the entire Universe resides.

I honor the place of love, of light, of truth, of peace.

I honor the place within you where if you are in that place in you,

and I am in that place in me, there is only one of us." ~
Baba Ram Dass, unk.

The Convergence

We are often quick to look at and frankly exploit the differences in our religious and faith beliefs and less apt to see the areas of similarity or commonality. But as history has demonstrated through wars, strife, discrimination, oppression and even genocide, this has not served us well. As referred in the introduction, perhaps our world and humankind would be much better off if we celebrated and honored those manners of faith and belief that we share and seek the divinity and sacredness inherent in each of us.

Pye (n.d.) offers three questions to provide a framework for a discussion as such:

1. Is there a basic outline, structure or shape that religions share?
2. Can we do a comparison of the various components and subsystems within different religions?
3. Are there different typologies or kinds of religions or is there a holistic typology?

The basic outline or structure that Pye (n.d.) delineates can be viewed through the lens of:

- the conceptual aspect or what people think, believe, or have in mind,
- what people do (the behavior),
- the social, that is the way people are grouped with each other, or relate to others
- finally, the subjective aspect of what people feel.

This paradigm parallels the previous notion of the various subsystems and components that help define our religious systems. Pye (n.d.) further shares that these four aspects may be significant for other realms of society and life which would include politics, business or even sports and education. These are, however all aspects that are reflected in some way in every religion. As is the nature of any system, if one of these aspects is overlooked, something important will be lacking in our understanding of a religion. For, like all systems, we must observe them as a total system within their environment.

Demarest (2009) offers an interesting perspective in his initial stage of spiritual development, that stage being *initial orientation*. In this it is suggested that as we "grow" into our beliefs -- that is reach a stage in our human developmental cycle wherein we can appreciate the nature of our spiritual beliefs as opposed to simply following the path of our parents -- that we first experience a form of jubilation or excitement and then we confront a series of challenges as we reflect on our life and life style.

In the Christian paradigm, those challenges would be an understanding of our *sins*. These would include: arrogance, greed, envy, selfish ambition, jealousy, hatred, anger, lust and love of money as the most significant. We can find similar references to such behaviors in virtually every other religious creed. To put these in context, they provide a framework for living and are at the core of most ethical systems. The behaviors manifest from some of these challenges form the basis of the other aspects of ethical systems.

Kurtz (2012) contends that every religious tradition has some set of interdependent beliefs, each woven in such a way as to reinforce the integrity of such beliefs; the fabric of this weave is dependent on each strand. These belief systems express world views that help societies (and associated sub sets) gain a perspective or picture of the way things are, the concept of nature, concept of society and concept of self -- thus in many ways defining the most comprehensive ideas of order. Kurtz (2012) goes further to share a perspective of the noted sociologist Emile Durkheim (c. 1915-1965) who contends that the entirety of human experience can be divided into two main categories, the *sacred* (that which is of ultimate concern) and the *profane* that which is ordinary and/or mundane. Contemporary thoughts on Durkheim's theory would place these two categories not as a dichotomy, but rather on a continuum. On this continuum, religions give an outlet for the celebration and understanding of the sacred through ritual or celebration and provide a foundation for the profane through teachings and principles of ethics on how one should live one's life.

The Shared

> *"Your beliefs become your thoughts,*
> *Your thoughts become your words,*
> *Your words become your actions,*
> *Your actions become your habits,*
> *Your habits become your values,*
> *Your values become your destiny."*
> **~ Mahatma Gandhi, unk**

For those that share a particular faith, specific times, places, items, and occasions are considered sacred. Most often these manners of sacredness are tied to the events that occurred "in the beginning" (Kurtz, 2012 p.25) and feature some ritual, re-creation or *re-actualization* of some sacred event. These beliefs systems are also systematized and disseminated by elite members of the religion, holy persons, priests, elders or holders of traditions,,and are reinforced by repetition. These beliefs are in fact incorporated into the speech, rhythm and pattern of everyday life and thus bridge the continuum to the profane.

Kuntz (2012) contends that religious beliefs are preserved through often contradictory stories and narratives most often in the abstract. He refers to this as the *cosmogony* that links the present to the past. These are the stories of life and death, good and evil, the divine and the human, all in existence side by side within the sacred stories. He makes a fascinating point in which he states "the world gets created twice in every culture" (p.

25). The first is in the material sense in which the world comes into being and the second is when it is re-created through the sacred stories or mythologies.

A few of these cosmogonies are categorized as follows:

- A God creates the world from a void
- Life springs forth from a cosmic egg
- A pre-chaotic being reaches in and pulls form up out of the water
- A mountain rises
- A giant being sustains the sky
- The world takes shape from and as a spiral
- A God delegates power to demi-gods or minor deities.

Further, most religions also have an *anthropogeny* or a theory of how humans came into being and how we should view ourselves.

Kuntz (2012) then posits that *theodicies* are how religions explain the presence of good and evil/ light and dark (dualistic theodicies), suffering, death and the like. As such, each faith path holds theories and mythologies about suffering including concepts of punishment for individual bad or sinful behavior, the result of natural processes, and the result of lessons not learned from previous lives, battles of good and evil, etc. These theodicies also frame concepts such as death and rebirth, wellness following illness, just rewards and such. Kuntz (2012) also shares the concept of *hierophany,* which is a term to identify and describe the way in which individuals encounter and experience the sacred, as well as *theophany,* a form of hierophany used to describe how individuals see sacredness manifest in other humans, e.g.; the Christ, Krishna, and angels. These terms (hierophany in particular) are also applied to the experience of seeing sacredness in nature (Moses and the burning bush from Judeo and Christian mythology) not unlike animistic mythology.

Of course the form of the experience of deity varies greatly from one path to another. Some forms (Abrahamic faiths in particular) profess a monotheistic view of deity. Other faiths are pantheistic or polytheistic. An interesting point offered by DiZerega (2001) in referring to the oft misunderstood polytheistic character of Pagan faiths is the notion of the *One* or the *Ultimate* Godhead are just an expression and an appreciation of the multifaceted manifestations of deity that are but parts of the *One*. Indeed many pantheistic faiths also hold sacredness in the *Ultimate* or *Supreme Being*, Zeus in the ancient Greek pantheon, Jupiter in ancient Roman and Indra in Hindu traditions are such examples. While espousing monotheistic beliefs, there is the example of the *Trinity* articulated in a few forms within Christian practices: the Father, Son and Holy Ghost; God the Father, the Virgin Mary the mother and the Christ child. Comparatively, there are many faiths that view the feminine and masculine not as dichotomies but as aspects of the *Ultimate* being.

Kuntz (2012) summarizes that religion is first and foremost a social phenomenon in that religious traditions grow out of and then feed the society in which it emerges. Secondly that religions, as expressed before, are a systematic set of beliefs that are acted upon and reinforced by rituals and the institution of religion itself; and finally that each faith constructs a religious ethos that sets and defines the ethical and taboo lines within a culture, defining those things that are acceptable vs. unacceptable behavior, defines identity, lends legitimacy to social order and gives the guidelines and framework for the profane or everyday life.

Pye (n.d.) then ponders if the various parts of different religions can be compared with and to one another. Some examples that might be enlightening question:

- If prayer in one religion is similar to prayer in another?
- Are there similar feelings or experiences when one enters a sacred place regardless of which religion holds it in sacredness?
- Are there venerated individuals of similar roles from one religion to another, e.g.; nuns, priests/priestesses, monks etc.? For instance,

similar to the Catholic church of Christian faith, Buddhist also upholds monks and nuns as holders of sacred traditions.

While these are common experiences of a spiritual awakening and alignment of sorts, there are other experiences that one has through the religious process. Demarest (2009), coins the concept of a "destabilizing of the soul" in which some manner of crisis interrupts ones steady state (p.43). This could be a sudden illness, financial crisis or other major life impact that is disruptive or disconcerting. He refers to this crisis as a *painful disorientation* and offers that these happenings illustrate just how fragile we humans are. Painful disorientations can also trigger a traumatic life transition. It is these types of issues that often drive one to seek religion or tries ones resolve in religion. These challenges test one's faith and resolve.

The traditions, rituals and teachings of religions become ever so important as a stabilizing factor when we as humans are disoriented and our faithful resolve is challenged. The use of prayer, meditation, reflection, visioning and other forms of patterned ritual provides a means by which humans seek to reorient from periods of painful disorientation. Kuntz (2012) provides a glimpse into the practices of Hindu and Buddhist practices and beliefs that offers examples of ritual work to balance practitioners.

The Hindu practice of yoga is one of many paths to enlightenment that involve some form of disciplined self-transcendence, all of which help one overcome excessive attachments to the mundane plane or earthly world. For reflective persons, one would employ <u>Jnana Yoga</u> or *The Path of Wisdom or Knowledge*. <u>Karma Yoga</u>, *The Path of Action* is for the active person and the most popular path <u>Bhaki Yoga </u>is *The Path of Devotion*. By choosing the *Path* that is most suitable to an individual's abilities and inclinations helps the believer transcend desires, selfishness and the routine of the profane.

Buddhist practitioners follow the *Four Nobel Truths* which are a series of propositions from the teachings of the Buddha: Life is Dukkha, typically translated as meaning suffering, anguish, or pain. Tanha (craving, attachment, desire) is the root of the suffering. One can overcome the Tanha and be released into *Nirvana* or the ultimate freedom in perfect existence. Finally, overcoming desire can be accomplished through the *Way* or the *Eightfold Path* to *Nirvana*. The *Eightfold Path* includes:

- Right knowledge or view
    - Sought in conjunction with the other seven attributes
- Right Aspiration
    - A Seeking of liberation with single-mindedness

- Right Speech
    - A mastery of one's use of language so as to move towards clarity, avoids abuse, slander, idle chatter, etc.
- Right Behavior
    - The essence of good moral behavior
- Right Livelihood
    - An avoidance of occupations that are incompatible with spiritual advancement
- Right Effort
    - Places importance on exertion and will
- Right Mindfulness
    - Places importance on the mind and its influence on one's life
- Right Concentration or Absorption
    - Using techniques from *Raja Yoga*

These may also be viewed in this paradigm:

Right View/knowledge   } Wisdom
Right Aspiration

Right Speech
Right Behavior   } Ethical Conduct
Right Livelihood

Right Effort
Right Mindfulness   } Mental development
Right Concentration/absorption

Another similarity of note is the practices surrounding the death of a family member. In Chinese traditions there is a ritual for seven days in which the decedents' son goes to a stream (flowing water) to offer his parents wine and "ghost money", this is symbolic for the decedent to use in the afterlife. In Jewish traditions, a seven day period (*Shiva*) is held wherein mourners (of 1st degree or immediate family) gather and experience an entire week of intense sadness.

During this period, extended family and friends gather and give love and attention to the needs of the bereaved. Jewish teachings hold that when a member of the community feels the heart-wrenching pain of grief, we should be there to comfort and console. Both of these exemplar rituals, in addition to sharing a seven day period of reflection and action, provides not only a period of mourning for the bereaved, but also hold sacred some manner of ritual to "see" the deceased to the "other side" or afterlife.

The Experience

The experience of the sacredness of place can be understood perhaps through the notion of spiritual travel or pilgrimage. Even Agnostics and Atheists have an appreciation for the value in such sites.

> "The world is filled with sacred sites - holy places that people believe or once believed to have

religious significance to them and their culture. These sacred sites are varied in their history, art, architecture, and meaning. Most have played some historical role; some continue to play a role in political, social, or cultural events. We can learn a lot about history, culture, art, and architecture by learning about sacred sites"

(Retrieved from http://atheism.about.com/od/religiousplaces/sacred_Sites_Profiles_of_Temples_Churches_Mosques_and_Sacred_Sites.htm)

The notion of sacred travel has very deep roots in human experience. It has origins in going to a specific spot to dance in circles as in most indigenous traditions and to when early humans would climb hilltops and mountains to be closer to God or the sky. There is reference in every sacred text and all verbal traditions of places of sacredness. A profound statement of one of many spiritual discoveries in Judaism is that all of us are pilgrims, strangers seeking Divinity. As such, even God's chosen as the Jewish tribes were considered, had to wander the wilderness to get their souls right.

Foxwood (2008), offers that every journey is defined by several stages:

- First, the purpose of the journey or what is it that moves one beyond the familiar,

- Secondly, the destination, where is it that one seeks to go,
- Third, the mechanism for travel, either through physical means (vehicles, walking, air flight) or metaphysical (through meditation, spiritual consciousness, transcendence) and
- Finally the integration of the journey or how one incorporates the shift and changes in both their spiritual and mundane/profane lives.

We find references that are full of the language of travel: processing and recessing (that is, moving in and out) from celebration and worship, walking the walk, following a divine path and our spiritual journeys of life. We find such reference even in popular music, "But I still haven't found what I'm looking for..." (Rock band U2, Rattle and Hum Album, 1988) Very often in ancient sites we find a wide-area circular action around the most sacred site. This may be a ceremonial dance (Native Americans), a worship service (Catholics), or a prayer or devotional walk (some Protestants; also the Islamic tawaf). This act of moving or standing in a circle reminds us and makes us aware that their life revolves around God and Divinity, and that we belong with others whose lives are also revolving around God.

Neo-Pagans often journey to archaeological or sacred ancient sites (such as ancient temples and stone circles) that are associated with pre-Christian religions and deities. Within the rationale of a Neo-Pagan worldview, several common understandings dissolve and reveal themselves as continuities at sacred sites: human body and earth body, the past and the present, inner and outer worlds, self and other, human and divinity, nature and sacred. There have been some efforts to build contemporary sacred sites throughout the U.S.; Four Quarters Farm on the East Coast is an example with the establishment of a sacred stone circle reminiscent of Stonehenge.

Through a process of a somatic experience and modes of attention (that is attending to and with one's body) in surroundings that frequently include the embodied presence of other pagan pilgrims, one experiences oneself not as isolated subjectivities living on Earth, but as sharing an inter-subjective experience with other pilgrims and with the Earth itself. (Rountree, 2006) Further, Rountree (2006) contends that for some, journeys to sacred pagan sites "potentially contribute to a radical re-inscription of the female body by exposing women to alternative representations of the feminine and by providing contexts in which the feminine can be re-imagined, re-experienced and performed differently through symbolic activity and ritual." (p., i)

Figure 8 shows artistic representations of the journey or the *Spiral Dance*.

The Spiral Mandala

Figure8 The Spiral Dance

Demarest (2009), shares a concept that aptly applies to the inter-subjective experience articulated above. Perhaps his notion of *"Joyful Re-orientation"* speaks to this experience. "As we worshipped, learned, shared and prayed together, I sensed the Spirit bearing me up on the Mount of Transfiguration to behold the glorified... I also sensed that I was being drawn back into the life of the church..." He finishes that passage stating the "God delights in seeing his children move from the darkness of painful disorientation to the light of joyful orientation." (p 127) This is a powerful passage in that is elucidates the experience held by many in visiting a place of sacredness or sharing a *"pilgrimage"*, the collective *and* individual experience in that of reconnection and some form of transfiguration, moving beyond the profane and connecting with Spirit. Now while here it is referenced to religious experience, the same holds true to agnostics and atheist in that an experience of connection with and being moved by a place or ritual or music or piece of art transcends faith or belief and simply connects one in a profound way in often unspeakable and life changing experiences.

The Path from Diversity to a Pluralistic Society

"There are many paths up the Mountain, but the view of the moon from the top is the same." ~ **Ancient Japanese saying**

For all of the diversity that is espoused in America, we are a far distance from true plurality, religious or otherwise. The notion of pluralism is at best ambiguous. You'll find reference to it as a synonym for religious diversity while at other times, it refers to the belief that truth exists equally in all faith traditions. For this discourse we will hold that plurality honors the profound truths in each and every faith path. Plurality is a wondrous experience that draws societies together despite diversity. It's not just an acceptance of the differences and the diversity but an honoring of that diversity and difference and celebrating, in the spiritual context, the richness and sacredness of each religious path and frankly equally valuing the non-religious path. Two examples stand out in a celebration of pluralism. One offered by pluralism.org,

> "On the same street in Silver Spring, Maryland the Vietnamese Catholic Church, the Cambodian Buddhist Temple, the Ukranian Orthodox Church, the Muslim Community Center, the Disciples of Christ Church and the Mangal Mandir Hindu Temple are all located in the same neighborhood."

(Retrieved from http://pluralism.org/pluralism/essays/from_diversity_to_pluralism.php)

As the second example nearby in Laurel, Maryland you can find within 1000 feet of each other, a synagogue, a mosque, a Baptist church, and a Seventh Day Adventist church. As delineated on pluralism.org, "This is certainly diversity, but without any engagement or relationship with one another it may not be an instance of pluralism". Simple proximity or détente may certainly represent a diverse community and mutual respect, but by no means implies that there is any manner of engagement or even collaboration. It would be wonderful if there was an engagement between the differing faiths, thus moving us towards a more just common society; but absent an appreciation of the richness of our various faiths and paths, this may be an elusive goal.

Knitter (1995) shares that a global consciousness emerged as the cold war between the U.S. and the former U.S.S.R. drew to a close. This consciousness opened the doors for dialogue on social, economic, ecological, famine/strife, and political issues. One of the areas that Knitter (1995) posits is that for instance, various dimensions of the emerging global environmental crisis, including the ethical and spiritual commitments at the root of many ecological problems became areas in which global cooperation could proliferate. Further, these matters open possibilities of a global ethic of responsibility in a religiously pluralistic world. Although the various issues facing the global community start in different places, Knitter contends that the dialogue can best be pursued by focusing on common problems of survival. He further proposes an ethical base in "eco-human well-being." This base can be a universal foundation on which all nations can agree on in carrying on their dialogue, despite their religious differences.

Perhaps most significant, Knitter (1995) rejects both religious exclusivism that sees Christianity as the only true faith and inclusivism that ultimately subsumes the good in every faith within the Christian orbit. Thus there is an affirmation of a radical pluralism of religions. This indeed is a radical departure from traditional teachings and a direct challenge to the imperialism with which Christianity has approached the world for centuries.

There have been three primary ways in which Americans have approached the ever-expanding religious and cultural diverseness: exclusion, assimilation and finally pluralism. For those that are exclusionists, the answer is to close the borders, which is to not allow anymore "aliens" in the country. In the 1930s and 40s it was Asians and Jews, today it is Muslims and Hispanics. For those who saw America as "the great melting pot," (assimilationists), new immigrants should leave their differences and angularities behind and become "like us", conforming to a overwhelmingly Christian culture. Pluralists however share the view that one should come as you are and would welcome all your differences and angularities with a pledge only to the common civic values and expectations of American citizenship. A pluralist appreciates the contribution of distinctive ways to the "orchestra" of American civilization. (Columbia University Press) Retrieved from http://pluralism.org/pluralism/essays/from_diversity_to_pluralism.php

    The Dalai Lama espouses that finding common ground among faiths can help bridge divides at a time when unification and unified action are more important than ever in human existence. He offers that "As a species, we must embrace the oneness of humanity as we face global issues like pandemics, economic crises and ecological disaster. At that scale, our response must be as one. Harmony among the major faiths has become an essential ingredient of peaceful coexistence in our world. From this perspective, mutual understanding among these traditions is not merely the business of religious believers — it matters for the welfare of humanity as a whole". (Many Faiths, One Truth Published: May 24, 2010   Tenzin Gyatso, the 14th Dalai Lama retrieved from: http://www.nytimes.com/2010/05/25/opinion/25gyatso.html?_r=1)

Baha'u'llah (the prophet of Baha'i teachings) has said in regards to the various religious systems that each have "principles and laws and that these firmly-established and mighty systems have all proceeded from one source, thus are the rays of a single light. That these paths differ from one another can be attributed to the varying requirements throughout history" . (Retrieved from http://info.bahai.org/article-1-4-0-4.html) Thus the principle of the unity of religion implies in part that all of the great religious founders and prophets--the Manifestations--have come from The Divine, and that all of the religious systems established by those prophets are part of a single divine plan directed by the Divine. These prophets or messengers (Baha'u'llah called them "Manifestations of God"), are principally the founders of the major revealed religions, such as Abraham, Moses, Buddha, Zoroaster, Jesus, Muhammad, etc.

Baha'u'llah shares that there is truly only one religion—that being of the Divine. As such, this one religion is continually evolving and each religious system represents a stage in the evolution of the whole. Sadly, many adherents of various religious traditions are emphatic that the prophet or founder of their particular tradition represents a true revelation of the Divine to humanity and that the other religious founders are false prophets, or at least essentially inferior to their own.

The primary and fundamental principle elucidated by Baha'u'llah that the followers of Baha'i firmly believe, is that religious truth is not absolute but relative, that Divine Revelation is a continuous and progressive process. Further Baha'u'llah holds that "all the religions of the world are divine in origin, that their basic principles can be harmony, that their purposes are one and the same, that their teachings are facets of one truth, that their functions are complementary, that they differ only in the nonessential aspects of their doctrines, and that their missions represent successive stages in the spiritual evolution of human society." (Retrieved from http://info.bahai.org/article-1-4-0-4.html)

So what then moves us closer to the notion of pluralism? First, as espoused by Columbia University Press (2006), pluralism is not simply the absolute fact of plurality or diversity alone, but instead is the active engagement with that diversity. We can observe or even "celebrate" and honor diversity. Conversely we can be threatened by it as so many are. Of course if one is threatened then simple human survival instincts emerge and one acts of out self-preservation and defense. This sad truth can be seen manifest in the current political climate in the U.S. and the bitter divide that is challenging our political structure and the structure and stability of some of the larger Christian denominations. To manifest true pluralism requires active participation and engagement.

Secondly, it requires far more than simple tolerance of differences. Pluralism requires us to have some knowledge of our differences. While it helps for one to be tolerant of differences, tolerance as articulated by Columbia University Press (2006) does little to remove our ignorance of difference. With the vast diversity of belief, faith and understanding in the U.S. alone, simply tolerating each other does little to open our appreciation of each other. In this regard, tolerance is a very thin veil that could and does easily give way to being threatened when we believe something or someone is encroaching on "our beliefs".

The third notion that Columbia puts forth is that pluralism is not simply relativism but instead makes room for real and different religious commitments. Some mistakenly think that a pluralist perspective assumes that there is no real difference among various religious traditions and their values; this is a false assumption. Pluralism acknowledges the differences and in fact celebrates them as part of a rich mosaic of beliefs. You see, from a pluralistic perspective, one's beliefs are not weakened by the exploration, understanding *and* appreciation of the beliefs of others, but frankly strengthened as we seek the commonalities and understand that there is far greater value in the diverseness of belief then in single-minded and simplistic dichotomies.

We are blessed with a profound guarantee of acceptance of a pluralistic society in the U.S. and that rests in the core ground rules of First Amendment to the

Constitution. It is best stated by Columbia University Press (2006) as follows:

> "Pluralism in America is clearly based on the common ground rules of the: 'no establishment' of religion and the 'free exercise' of religion. The vigorous encounter of a pluralistic society is not premised on achieving agreement on matters of conscience and faith, but achieving a vigorous context of discussion and relationship. E Pluribus Unum, 'out of many, one' ; envisions one people, a common sense of a civic 'we', but not one religion, one faith, one conscience. Unum does not mean uniformity. Perhaps the most valuable thing people of many faiths have in common is their commitment to a society based on the give and take of the civil dialogue at a common table".

(Retrieved from http://pluralism.org/pluralism/essays/from_diversity_to_pluralism.php)

Finally, Columbia suggests that we must nurture a constructive dialogue towards pluralism that reveals both the common understandings and real differences amongst our beliefs. A true dialogue does not imply that everyone will agree with one another and indeed there should be lively debate. The debate should reveal our areas of convergence and those of divergence but most importantly, must be done from a place of mutual respect. The notion of pluralism requires us to commit to even engaging in the dialogue. So often, the conversation is drowned out by fear, irrational belief, ethnocentrism and the intolerance mentioned before. We must, as Columbia suggests, discover "where the metaphorical 'tables' are in American society" and make a commitment to being at the *'table'* to engage in true dialogue. That then sets the stage for true pluralism.

The Dalai Lama articulates best with this passage:

> "Granted, every religion has a sense of exclusivity as part of its core identity. Even so, I believe there is genuine potential for mutual understanding. While preserving faith toward one's own tradition, one can respect, admire and appreciate other traditions.
>
> An early eye-opener for me was my meeting with the Trappist monk Thomas Merton in India shortly before his untimely death in 1968. Merton told me he could be perfectly faithful to Christianity, yet learn in depth from other religions like Buddhism. The same is true for me as an ardent Buddhist learning from the world's other great religions.
>
> A main point in my discussion with Merton was how central compassion was to the message of both Christianity and Buddhism. In my readings of the New Testament, I find myself inspired by Jesus' acts of compassion. His miracle of the loaves and

fishes, his healing and his teaching are all motivated by the desire to relieve suffering.

And I've learned how the Talmud and the Bible repeat the theme of compassion, as in the passage in Leviticus that admonishes, "Love your neighbor as yourself."

(Many Faiths, One Truth Published: May 24, 2010 Tenzin Gyatso, the 14th Dalai Lama retrieved from: http://www.nytimes.com/2010/05/25/opinion/25gyatso.html?_r=1)

There is a profound beauty in the diverse and pluralistic manifestations of faith and belief. It is like a mosaic of fine art, open for appreciation, absent prejudice and a wondrous cacophony of richness, diversity, culture and lessons. One must only open one's self to appreciate that fullness and gain from the experience. One of the simplest commonalities is the ethical precepts and constructs that religions hold. In those principles of life, we find the most profound and binding ties that we all share. While our paths to the Divine and our interpretation of the 'mosaic of fine art' might differ, we converge on how we should treat one another. Perhaps there is the starting point for a world of plural understanding.

The Ethical Richness

Wiccans hold to a single but profound standard for guiding behavior, the *Wiccan Rede.* The Rede (as defined on Dictionary.com) "is a statement that provides the key moral system in the Neopagan religion of Wicca and other related faiths". The most common form of the Rede is '*An it harm none, do what ye will*'. What does this mean? Simply put, you can do whatever you want to as long as it harms no one or nothing --including yourself. It is a simple belief that constantly reminds us that there are many consequences to our actions and as such we **must** consider all possible outcomes before acting. The Wiccan Rede thereby binds Wiccans to do the right thing.

The second profound guiding principle is that of the Three-fold law based in part on the articulated laws of Karma that states that any good that a person does to another returns to themselves, magnified three times. On the same notion any harm also returns in the same 3:1 ratio. This provides strong motivation for one to behave ethically and to avoid doing or causing harm to others. These two principles are not unlike the ethical rule from other faiths. Buddhist ethics, according to Kurtz (2012) espouses The Five Precepts: Do not kill, do not steal, do not lie, do not be unchaste (different meaning implied for holy people and the mundane) and finally do not drink intoxicants. Abrahamic faiths have the Ten Commandments (although in a slightly different form for

Islamic believers) and the "Golden Rule" paraphrased here as "do unto others as you would have done unto you." Confucianism has the "Silver Rule" which holds "Do not do to others what you would not like them to do to you" and espouses filial piety (a obedience, care and respect for one's parents and ancestors). Islam calls for compassion, a love of God, and a showing of mercy to all creation.

Table 2 presents a comparative view of what shall be called *The Rules of 10*. These rules or laws from different faith paths illuminate guiding principles from the various faiths and are modeled on the Ten Commandments of the Abrahamic faiths which is also shown. Of note is that all of the Abrahamic faiths share the commandments, though the Islamic faith has a slight modification on the original text.

Table 2 The Rules of 10

The Rules of 10

Wiccan/Pagan	Abrahamic	Islamic (derivation)	Native American	Buddhist	Confucian
Thou art God/Goddess	I am the LORD thy God	There is no God except one God	The earth is our mother, care for her	Abstain from harming living beings	Respect the old, educate the young, and trust your friends.
As above, so below. As within, so without	Thou shalt not take the name of the Lord thy God in vain	There is nothing whatsoever like unto Him	Honor all your relations	Abstain from taking things not freely given	Do not do to others what you would not have them do to you
Spirit abides in all things. Words and names have meaning	Remember thou keep the Sabbath Day	Make not God's name an excuse to your oaths	Open your heart and soul to the Great Spirit	Abstain from sexual misconduct	Great man sets the good example, then he invites others to follow it
Maintain an attitude of gratitude	Honor thy Father and thy Mother	Be kind to your parents if one or both of them attain old age in thy life...	All life is sacred: treat all beings with respect	Abstain from false speech	Shall I tell you what knowledge is? It is to know both what one knows and what one does not know.
Honor the Ancestors, teachers, elders, and leaders.	Thou shalt not kill	As for the thief, male or female, cut off his or her hands, but those who repent After a crime and reform shall be forgiven by God...	Take from the Earth what is needed and nothing more	Abstain from intoxicants (drugs/alcohol)	Humanity-at-its-best: At home be humble, at work be respectful, and with others be loyal.
All life is sacred.	Thou shalt not commit adultery	They invoke a curse of God if they lie.	Do what needs to be done for the good of all	Abstain from taking untimely meals	Society is not an adversarial system based on contractual relationship, but is a community of trust with emphasis on communication.
All acts of love and pleasure are sacred.	Thou shalt not steal	If anyone has killed one person it is as if he had killed the whole mankind	Give constant thanks to the Great Spirit for each new day	Abstain from dancing, singing music and watching grotesque mime	A political culture based on responsibility and trust is politics with moral persuasion.
Whatever you send out returns threefold.	Thou shalt not bear false witness against thy neighbor	Do not come near adultery. It is an indecent deed and a way for other evils	Speak the truth; but only of the good in others	Abstain from the use of garlands, perfumes, adornments	Great man demands it of himself; petty man of others.
Love is the law. Love under will.	Thou shalt not covet thy neighbor's wife	Saying of the Prophet Muhammad (P.) "One of the greatest sins is to have illicit sex with your neighbors wife".	Follow the rhythms of nature; rise and retire with the sun	Abstain from use of high seats	You can always learn from three people in the street, take up the good and improve the bad.
For the greatest good, "An' it harm none."	Thou shalt not covet thy neighbor's goods	When the call for the Friday Prayer is made, hasten to the remembrance of God and leave off your business	Enjoy life's journey, but leave no tracks	Abstain from accepting silver or gold	Remain sincere in purpose while studying widely, continue to think while posing frank and open questions. Therein lies Manhood-at-its-best.

Moving forward

On the Wiccan and Pagan path, there is an amazing relationship between our beliefs and the nature of reality and how we behave. This accordingly, holds true in both our secular and spiritual beliefs. (DiZerega, 2001) It goes to reason then that we can and *should* appreciate the diverseness of nature (and by extension humans and human existence). But as we observe and honor the vast and collective differences in nature, we also behold and stand witness to the harmony that exists as well. There are three major ways in which DiZerega (2001) contends that we differ most from the largest faith group, Christianity:

- Religious Pluralism- the recognition and respect of many spiritual paths and faiths
- An emphasis on harmony rather than salvation as a primary religious focus
- A greater respect and appreciation of one's personal experience of spirit rather than faith or the experience of others as validation of spiritual truths

These differences are real and in some ways profound but as DiZerega (2001) contends, there is a respect and regard for the world and nature in Christian teachings and as such there is a harmony in the greatest insights within that path and that of paganism. Wicca and paganism are not Christianity or Zoroastrianism or Buddhism but these paths are complimentary and can harmonize. A profound statement shares "to the degree we can incorporate these insights into our lives; we come to a deeper harmony with the Divine". Such Harmony teaches us patience, kindness, compassion, and understanding. From such a foundation, deep and profound lives can emerge. (DiZerega, 2001 p. 228)

Adler (2006) shares that Pagans and Wiccans have been embracing interfaith work like no other time before. With a presence at the Parliament of World Religions and events like the Ecumenicon Interfaith Conference near Washington, DC, Pagans have increased presence and are moving for a wider acceptance as one of the world's growing religions. Gulen (2004) offers a powerful analogy paraphrased to say that humans are the greatest mirror of the names, deeds, and many attributes of the divine, a mirrored reflection and a marvelous fruit of life that has the power to alter its destiny, relations and environs. It would seem then that with the bountiful blessings given to us to care for and marvel--that we humans would harness the power given us to collectively move forward. Much needs to be done for us to reach the potential that every religious path says we should aspire. Much needs to be done for us to *"reach the mountain top"* but perhaps in our collective journey, our pilgrimage and travel of the circle, we will learn the lesson that all travelers eventually come to understand—we are not on the path alone, others have trod this path before--to reach the peak, the lessons, guidance and wisdom of others will be necessary.

> *"If Humanity is the vicegerent of God on Earth, the favorite of all His creation, the essence and substance of existence in its entirety and the brightest mirror of the creator—and there is no doubt that this is so—then the Divine Being that has sent humanity to this realm will have us give the right, permission and ability to discover the mysteries imbedded in the soul of the universe, to uncover hidden power, might and potential, to use everything to its purpose, and to be the representatives of characteristics that belong to Him…"*

~ M. Fethullah Gulen, (2004)

This written journey has taken us through the history of religion and examined the impact of faith and belief on society. In this we have also explored the convergences and divergences of our beliefs and faiths. We've examined theologies and the use of theologies to understand one another and appreciate the paths that we traverse.

We looked at those areas of ethical considerations and foundations and we explored the ultimate journey, that which takes us closer to the Divine. It is my hope that the text of this may be a guidepost to help move the process of a pluralistic understanding forward. It is my sincere wish that we can, as Gulen suggests, exemplify and be the vicegerent of *God (Goddess) on Earth*. Forward now with the help of the Gods to a true pluralistic, loving, caring society.

References

About.com. (n.d.). *Sacred Sites Profiles*. Retrieved 5 1, 2012, from atheist.about.com: http://atheism.about.com/od/religiousplaces/Sacred_sites_Profiles_of_Temples_Churches_Mosques_and_Sacred_Sites.htm

Adherants.com. (n.d.). *Major Religions of the World Ranked by number of Adherants*. Retrieved 2 17, 2012, from www.adheratns.com: http://www.adherants.com/Religions_by_Adherants.html

Adler, M. (2006). *Drawing Down the Moon; Witches Druids, Goddess-Worshipers and other Pagans in America*. New York: Penguin.

Baha'i International Community. (2012). *Baha'i The Oneness of Religion*. Retrieved 2 17, 2012, from Bahai' Topics: http://info.bahai.org/article-1-4-0-4.html

Blummer, H. (1969). *Symbolic Interactionism. Perspective and method*. Out of Print.

Bowker, J. (2006). *World Religion*. New York: DK Publishing, Inc.

Brown, C. (2007). *Natural or Supernatural*. Retrieved 04 22, 2012, from Indiana University News INfo: http://newsinfo.iu.edu/web/page/normal/4779.html

Brownstein, T. (2001). *The Interfaith Prayer Book*. uknown: self published- direibuted by www.interfaithresources.com.

Chaves, M. (Summer 2011). Religious Trends in America. *Social Work and Chrisitanity 38.2* , 119-132.

Columbia University Press. (2006). *On Common Ground: World Religions in America.* Retrieved 5 2, 2012, from Pluralism.org: http://pluralism.org/pluralism/essays/from_diverity_to_pluralism.php

Davies-Stofka, B. (n.d.). *Patheos: Christianity overview and history.* Retrieved 3 1, 2012, from Patheos Website: http://www.patheos.com/Library/Christianity.html

Davies-Stofka, B., & Fadel, M. (n.d.). *Patheos: Islam origins, history and overview.* Retrieved 3 2, 2012, from Patheos Website: http://www.patheos.com/Library/Islam.html

Davies-Stofka, B., Mulhern, K. A., & Kinnard, J. N. (n.d.). *Patheos: Jehovah's Witnesses.* Retrieved 3 25, 2012, from Jehovas Witnessess Overview: http://www.patheos.com/Library/Jehovahs-Witnesses.html

Demarest, B. A. (2009). *Seasons of the Soul: Stages of Spiritual Development.* Downers Grove, Il: InterVarsity Press.

Dictionary.com. (n.d.). *dictionary.com/reference.* Retrieved 4 3, 2012, from definition of religion: http://dictionary.reference.com/browse/religion

Dirks, J. F. (2004). *The Abrahamic Faiths: Judaism, Christianity, and Islam Similarities and Contrasts.* Beltsville, MD: amana publications.

diZerega, G. (2001). *Pagans & Christians: The Personal Spiritual Experience.* Woodbury, MN: Llewellyn Publications.

Douglas, S. (n.d.). *Historical Background: The Abrahamic Faiths*. Retrieved 3 2, 2012, from http://www.islamicspain.tv: http://www.islamicspain.tv/For-Teachers/8_Historical%20Background%20The%20Abrahamic%20Faiths.pdf

Dowling, E. M., Scarlett, W. G., & eds. (2006). *Encyclopedia of Religious and Spiritual Development.* Thousand Oaks: Sage Publications.

Droogers, A. (2005). Syncretism and Fundamentalism: A Comparison. *Social Compass vol. 52 no. 4*, 463-471.

Faiver, C., Ingersoll, R. E., O'Brien, E., & McNally, C. (2001). *Explorations in Counseling and Spirituality: Philosophical, Practical and Personal Reflections.* Belmont: Brooks/Cole Thomson Learning.

Farrar, J., & Farrar, S. (1996). *The Witches' Bible: The Complete Witches' Handbook.* Blaine, WA: Phoenix Publishing.

Flere, S. (2007). Gender and Religious Orientation. *Social Compass 2007 vol. 54 no 2.*, 239-253.

Foxwood Temple. (1989). *Book of Laws.* Laurel: self published.

Foxwood, O. (2007). *The Faery Teachings.* Berkeley: R J Stewart Books.

Foxwood, O. (2008). *The Tree of Enchantment: Ancient Wisdom and Magic Practices of the Faery Tradition.* San Fransico: Red Wheel/Weiser.

Gill, R., Mann, G., Mulhern, K., & Kinnard, J. N. (n.d.). *Patheos: Sikhism Overview*. Retrieved 2 27, 2012, from Patheos website: http://www.patheos.com/Library/Sikhism.html

Grim, J. A. (n.d.). *Inrtoduction to Indigenous Traditions; Indigenous Traditions and Ecology*. Retrieved 3 21, 2012, from Yale University: http://fore.research.yale.edu/religion/indigenous/

Gunn, J. (n.d.). *Patheos: Jainism*. Retrieved 3 12, 2012, from Patheos Website: http://www.patheos.com/Library/Jainism.html

Gyatso, T. (2010, 5 24). Many Faiths, One Truth. *The New York Times* , p. Op Ed.

Hardy, J. (n.d.). *Patheos: Seek and Understand, Buddhism Overview*. Retrieved 3 15, 2012, from www.patheos.com/Library.html: http://www.patheos.com/Library/Buddhism.html

Harvard Unvieristy Pluralsism Project. (n.d.). *From Diversity to Pluralism*. Retrieved 2 17, 2012, from The Pluralism Project at Harvard University Web site: http://pluralism.org/pluralism/essays/from_diversity_to_plurali sm.php

International World History Project. (n.d.). *The religious beliefs and practices of the ancient Celts*. Retrieved 3 26, 2012, from World History Project: http://history-world.org/celts%20religious_beliefs_and_practices_.htm

Khalek, N., Mulhern, K. A., & Kinnard, J. N. (n.d.). *Sufism Overview.* Retrieved 3 25, 2012, from Patheos.com: http://www.patheos.com/Library/Sufism-x3993.html

Kinnard, J. (n.d.). *Patheos Hinduism Overview.* Retrieved 3 15, 2012, from Patheos Website: http://www.patheos.com/Library/Hinduism.html

Knitter, P. F. (1995). *One Earth, Many Religions: Multifaith Dialogue and Global Responsibility.* Maryknoll, NY: Orbis Books.

Knitter, P. F. (1995). *One Earth, Many Religions: Multifaith Dialogue and Global Responsibility.* Maryknoll, NY: Orbis Books.

Krell, M. A., & Nadler, A. (n.d.). *Patheos: Judaism History.* Retrieved 2 29, 2012, from Patheos Website: http://www.patheos.com/Library/Judaism.html

Kurtz, L. R. (2012). *Gods in the Global Village; The World's Religions in Sociological Perspective.* Los Angeles: Sage Publiations, .

Marx, K. (2012, 4 3). Quotation "opiate of the masses". http://en.wikipedia.org/wiki/Opium_of_the_people.

McColman, C. (n.d.). *Patheos.com: Paganism.* Retrieved 3 27, 2012, from Paganism overview: www.patheos.com/Library/Paganism.html

Melton, J. G. (n.d.). *Patheos: Scientology.* Retrieved 3 27, 2012, from Sceintology: http://www.patheos.com/Library/Scientology.html

Momen, M. (n.d.). *Patheos: Baha'i.* Retrieved 3 22, 2012, from Baha'i overview: http://www.patheos.com/Library.Bahai.html

Ontario Consultants on Religions Tolerance. (n.d.). *Religions of the World: Information about forty organized religions and faith groups.* Retrieved 2 19, 2012, from Religious Tolerance.org: http://www.religioustolerance.org/var_rel.htm

Ontario Consultants on Religious Tolerance. (n.d.). *Wicca: Wiccan Terminology.* Retrieved 3 28, 2012, from http://www.religioustolerance.org/wic_term.htm

Opera Pia International. (1982). *Aging: Spiritual Perspectives.* Lake Worth: Sunday Publications, Inc.

Patheos. (n.d.). *Patheos: Seek and Understand.* Retrieved 2 21, 2012, from Patheos Website: http://www.patheos.com/Library/Religions-Traditions-Faiths.html

Patheos.com. (n.d.). *Africa.* Retrieved 3 22, 2012, from Patheos.com/African.html: http://www.patheos.com/Library/Africa.html

Patheos.com. (n.d.). *Afro-Brazilian.* Retrieved 3 19, 2012, from Patheos.com/Library: http://www.patheos.com/Library/Afro-Brazilian.html

Patheos.com. (n.d.). *Afro-Caribean.* Retrieved 3 19, 2012, from Patheos.com/Library: http://www.patheos.com/Library/Afro-Caribbean.html

Patheos.com. (n.d.). *Christian Sceince Overview.* Retrieved 3 26, 2012, from patheos.com: Christian Science: http://www.patheos.com/Library/Christian-Science.html

Patheos.com. (n.d.). *Indigenous religions: Australian*. Retrieved 3 20, 2012, from Patheos.com: http://www.patheos.com/Library/Australia.html

Patheos.com. (n.d.). *Korea Overview*. Retrieved 3 15, 2012, from Patheos.com: http://www.patheos.com/Korea.html

Patheos.com. (n.d.). *North America Overview*. Retrieved 3 18, 2012, from Patheos.com/North-America: http://www.patheos.com/Library/North-America.html

Patheos.com. (n.d.). *Oceania Overview*. Retrieved 3 21, 2012, from Patheos.com: http://www.patheos.com/Library/Oceania.html

Patheos.com. (n.d.). *Patheos.com South America Indigenous*. Retrieved 3 19, 2012, from patheos.com/South America: http://www.patheos.com/Library/South-America.html

Patheos.com. (n.d.). *Patheos.com; Germanic overview*. Retrieved 3 25, 2012, from Patheos.com: http://www.patheos.com/Library/Germanic.html

Patheos.com. (n.d.). *Patheos: Unitarian-Universalism*. Retrieved 3 26, 2012, from Unitarian-Universalist Overview: http://www.patheos.com/Library/Unitarian-Universalism.html

Pew Forum on Religion & Public Life. (2011, 2). *Faith in Flux report*. Retrieved 2 18, 2012, from Pew Forum Web site: http://www.pewforum.org/Faith-in-Flux.aspx/

Pew Forum. (2009, 12 9). *Other Beliefs and Practices*. Retrieved 2 18, 2012, from Pew Forum Web site: http://www.pewforum.org/Other-Beliefs-and-Practices/Many-Americans-Mix-Multiple-Faiths.aspx

Pye, M. (n.d.). *Patterns of Comparative Religion*. Retrieved 2 20, 2012, from Philospohy, Theology and Religion (PhilTar): http://www.philtar.ac.uk/encyclopedia/introd.html

Richey, J. (n.d.). *Patheos: Seek , Understand: Confucianism Overview*. Retrieved 3 21, 2012, from Patheos Web site: http://www.patheos.com/Library/Confucianism.html

Roberts, K. A., & Yamane, D. (2012). *Religion in Sociological Pespective*. Los Angeles: Sage:Pine Forge.

Rountree, K. (2006 v.12). Performing the Divine: Neo-Pagan Pilgrimages and Ebmbodiment at Sacred Sites. *Body and Society* , 95-115.

Rubinstein, M. (n.d.). *Encyclopedia Britannica*. Retrieved 3 27, 2012, from New Religeous Movement: http://www.britannica.com/EBchecked/topic/1007307/new-religious-movement-NRM

Silver Web Raithe. (1983). *Book of Traditions*. Baltimore: Self Published.

Space and Motion. (n.d.). *Theology; Summary & History of World Religions. On Morality, Free Will and God*. Retrieved 2 18, 2012, from Space and Motion; On Truth and Reality; The spherical standing wave structure of matter in space: http://www.spaceandmotion.com/theology-morality-god-world-religions.htm

Starhawk, M. S. (1999). *The Spiral Dancde; A rebirth of the Ancient Religion of the Goddess*. New York: HarperCollins.

Taylor, R. J., Chatters, L. M., Jayakody, R., & Levin, J. S. (1996). Black and White Differences in Religious Participation: A

Multisample Comparison. *Journal for the Scientific Study of Religion vol. 35 issue 4* , 403-411.

The Holy Bible. (1978). *The Holy Bible, KJV.* The National Publishing Co.

The Koran. (2004). *The Koran (Qur'an): Based on the original english translations of J.M. Rodwell.* New York: Bantam Dell.

The Sunni Forum. (n.d.). *The Sunni Forum website*. Retrieved 2 20, 2012, from The Sunni Forum website: http://www.sunniforum.com/forum/forum.php

U2 (Composer). (1988). Rattle and Hum. [U2, Performer] Island Records.

Vaughns-1-pagers. (n.d.). *Religions Summary - Compares Major religions*. Retrieved 2 19, 2012, from Vaughns Summaries: http://www.vaughns-1-pagers.com/religion/religions-summary.htm

Wilkinson, P. J., & Coleman, P. G. (2010). Strong beliefs adn coping in old age: a case based comparision of atheism and religious faith. *Ageing nad Society Vol. 30 No.2* , 337-361.

Yavuz, M. H., & Esposito, J. L. (2003). *Turkish Islam and the Secular State: The Gulen Movement.* Syracuse: Syracuse University Press.

Zaidman, N., Goldstein-Gidoni, O., & Nehemya, I. (2009). From Temples to Organizaions: The Introduction and Packaging of Spirituality. *Organization vol. 16 No. 4* , 597-621.

Zeller, B. E. (n.d.). *Patheos: ISKCON*. Retrieved 3 25, 2012, from ISKCON (Hare Krishna) Overview:

http://www.patheos.com/Library/ISKCON-%28Hare-Krishna%29.html

Zeller, B. E. (n.d.). *Patheos:New Age*. Retrieved 3 26, 2012, from New Age: http://www.patheos.com/Library/New-Age.html

www.ingramcontent.com/pod-product-compliance
Lightning Source LLC
Chambersburg PA
CBHW030235170426
43201CB00006B/224